"My intention for this book is to assist

you great Creator Beings that are

My spark of light and love

to easily shift out of duality

and back home into one love,

one light, and one heart!"

~ Message from the CREATOR ~

∞

THE CREATOR HEALS

5 DNA ACTIVATORS

5 SIMPLE KEYS TO LIVING A LIFE OF COMPLETE FREEDOM

Michelle Phillips

Michelle Phillips
Sedona, AZ
(928) 821-2038
www.soulsawakening.net

ISBN 978-0-692-39411-3

Printed in the United States of America

Cover art and book design by Mark Gelotte
www.markgelotte.com

A Dedication of Gratitude

I *am so grateful for all of you, my Soul Brothers and Sisters who have agreed to be on the Earth at this time of Ascension, to collectively awaken into ONE heart and ONE love to assist in shifting the consciousness of our world. I am grateful for everything that you agreed to go through to bring us to this place of our collective Souls' Awakening.*

I am grateful for my Swedish spiritual family, for their continual love, support and encouragement. Together, we have held the love and light for one another to move beyond our karmic agreements and stories.

I am grateful for my biological family, my four siblings, three children and grandchildren and of course my Parents for agreeing to give me all of the lessons that I needed to learn, to be able to return to my Soul's highest consciousness. We don't all have the same consciousness and spiritual beliefs, but we do have the highest truth of all, which is Love and support for one another and the ability to see great humor in our differences and to be able to laugh through some of life's challenges and our own shortcomings.

I am grateful for my editor, Julie ... what a fabulous job she has done! I write everything in long hand, and she has to make sense of my scribbling and type it together. This book would not be without her. I am grateful for my graphic artist, Mark. He is so tuned into Spirit and very easy, loving, and humble to work with.

I am grateful for my high spiritual team that has always been with me and has guided and supported me beyond who I thought I was or could be (like writing this book).

I am grateful to wake up in the morning filled so full of love, gratitude, and grace. I am grateful to wake up to the birds singing and to be able to look out at the trees and nature.

I am grateful to live in Sedona AZ, one of the highest spiritual meccas of the world. I am grateful to be surrounded by so many incredible Beings of like consciousness.

And ... beyond anything that I could conceive or think would happen, I am grateful that the "Source of Creation" has chosen me to bring forth to the world incredible downloads of knowledge and wisdom, first with "The Creator Speaks," "Teaches," and now these simple yet powerful five healing techniques: "The Creator Heals," DNA shifting, healing, and reprogramming.

I am grateful to get to the place in my own life where I feel and know that I have so much to be grateful for, to live from a place of gratitude, love, and grace. I am grateful!!!!!

Namaste,
Michelle

CONTENTS

Michelle's Introduction ix

Love's Awakening 1

Creator's Introduction 9

Chapter 1: The Creator - What is DNA? **15**

Chapter 2: Michelle's Story **23**

Chapter 3: The Collective DNA's Match and Merge **36**

Chapter 4: Pineal Gland's DNA Connection to Source **50**

Chapter 5: Pineal Gland Activation **55**

Chapter 6: Creator/Earth Grounding Technique **63**

Chapter 7: Collective DNA Matching **68**

Chapter 8: The Matching Process **83**

Chapter 9: How to Match Love: **89**

Chapter 10: Forgiveness **94**

Chapter 11: Heart/Soul: Theta HealingTechnique **101**

Chapter 12: Theta State **115**

Chapter 13: The Creator's Message: **118**

Chapter 14: Review of the Five Techniques **128**

Chapter 15: Michelle's Healing Journey **137**

About the Author *143*

"As your DNA is matching my DNA,

memories of your own love,

magnificence, inner power, and

purpose are being activated."

~ Message from the CREATOR ~

∞

MICHELLE'S INTRODUCTION

The Creator Heals – All I can say is, "Wow! Thank you Creator/Source for these very simple but profound healing techniques!" When I was asked by the Creator to write a very small book to give others the techniques to very quickly heal and shift their DNA from karmic, ancestral systems and patterns of sickness, dis-ease, conflict, and fear, I felt very excited. I felt excited to show people how to heal and shift their DNA into love, light, health, grace, prosperity, gratitude, forgiveness, and whatever else their desire may be.

It gives a person a great sense of inner peace and empowerment to be the Master of their own life – to be able to Co-Create your Soul's higher purpose on the Earth plane now.

I have been working with DNA re-patterning and re-programming since 2007. After healing myself from cancer through DNA healing and Soul Retrieval, I started using the healing processes in my workshops and have witnessed miraculous healings with others on all levels.

All of the healing work that I assist others with comes through my own healing process. I know the techniques work because they have continued to shift me from patterns, programs, sickness, and dis-ease and heal my life. I felt honored to be able to bring these simple, easy, and profound healing techniques to others.

I thought the book would be done in about three weeks.

What a surprise I had coming. I should have remembered from giving birth to our first book, "The Creator Speaks," that the Creator/Source was going to take me through another incredible healing journey.

I had forgotten about the labor pains one goes through in giving birth. The labor itself can be very painful and challenging, but once the birth takes place, the overwhelming love certainly outweighs the journey to get there.

I am very grateful to have been taken through this healing journey to be able to bring these amazing DNA techniques to you.

These simple DNA healing techniques will assist you to tap into and turn on your own inner power, light, and self love. You will tap into the collective DNA systems of love and awaken into your own divine love to live your life from your higher self's wisdom and knowledge.

Using the DNA healing tools will shift your DNA and give you the possibility to Co-Create the life you have always wanted and dreamed of.

You will learn to easily and effortlessly manifest your greatest desires and goals by matching and merging your collective DNA system with the morphogenetic field of your intentions.

As you awaken and merge into the higher vibrations of your own love multi-dimensionally, your lens of perception will shift into one of gratitude and grace.

You will start seeing, experiencing, and vibrating from

the morphogenetic field of the higher consciousness of God-Creator-Source energy. You will move out of communicating from your emotions or pain body to communicating in the highest and best for all.

When I originally began writing this book with the Creator, I thought we were only going to teach how to match and merge your etheric body's DNA system with your intentions. The Creator had a larger intention. His/Her intention was to teach me three more healing techniques through my own healing process. The Creator knew that when I experienced how easy and yet powerful the healing techniques were I would share them with you.

This book is written in layman's terms for all to experience and understand without the use of scientific or technical terms to explain the DNA. I am writing the book from my own experience and in the way the Creator wants it written. As I mentioned, all of the spiritual work that comes through me to assist others comes from my own healing experience. Because of this, I know that the healing modalities work. I am excited to be able to assist you with the **"Heart's Love Healing"** technique. It is a very simple, powerful technique that anyone can learn and do for themselves. We will also teach you the **Creator/Earth Grounding** technique and how to open and activate your **"Pineal Gland,"** your DNA connection to the wisdom and knowledge of the Source of Creation. Later in writing the book, the Creator brought through me the **"Heart Soul/Theta Healing"** technique, which I will also share with you.

So my beautiful Soul brothers and sisters, I am honored to collaborate with the Creator to bring to you the **"Collective DNA Matching"** and the *four* other healing modalities that the Creator shared with me through writing this book. As I mentioned, these simple healing tools will assist you to open your own heart's divine love and to match, and merge your DNA systems with the morphogenetic fields of your intentions.

Your inner balance of love will assist to Co-Create heaven on Earth, to shift the collective DNA system of the world out of fear and into love, harmony, peace, and Oneness.

While writing this book, I went through an incredible DNA healing, which I will share with you in the back of the book.

∞

LOVE'S AWAKENING

I have had so many incredible experiences of love, both on the Earth plane and with Spirit. I believe our Soul's journey on the Earth is to awaken into the sacredness and expansiveness of love. From the heart of love, all is forgivable. In the heart of love, we will experience life from the higher Knowing of all Soul's agreements here on the Earth. From this non-judgmental state, we will have compassion for others' journeys and will be able to hold the light and love for them without the need to try to fix the situation. We may assist by holding love, light, and compassion.

I believe our love's journey is a continual process of peeling away old layers of fear, of what is not love. Every layer we peel away brings us closer to our own divine love's essence. Love is our essence, our Creation, and we are now rebirthing ourselves into the memory, experience, and expression of love.

For many years as a child and young adult, I did not know what love was or what it felt like. I am so elated and grateful in my life now to experience love for and from others and to know that God/Creator's love is my true essence and guiding light.

I work with so many people like myself who have come into this lifetime with the absence of love in their lives. In healings, I will ask them if they can feel the love and they look at me with a frozen, blank stare. They don't know the feeling of love because they have not experienced it in this lifetime.

As soon as we activate and open their Pineal Gland DNA system into Mother/Father's love, their bodies open up to the memory and safety of love. From this safety, love's pure Source energy fills and floods them with the higher vibrational love.

When the body and heart feel safe to open to the memory and experience of love, it will expand, open up, and receive more love. Love is our heart and Soul's true essence. When you open to the safety of love, the subconscious along with the heart will open you to many more magical memories of love. If your intention is to match and merge with love, you may also find yourself shifting through the veils to release the emotions of what is not love. When you choose to awaken into your true essence of love, a coding in your DNA will activate and download a higher frequency of light. This higher frequency of light will start moving through the multi-dimensional layers or veils of your hurtful emotions connected to love. As your magnificent light activates the frozen emotions that need to be healed and released, you may experience yourself on an emotional roller coaster ride. This emotional ride can be referred to as a "Dark Night of the Soul" experience. All Beings of light shift through the dark night in their Souls' awakening. It is an initiation process. There is a light at the end of the tunnel. As you move through the tunnel, you will emerge back into a higher light and understanding within yourself.

From the release of your frozen emotions, your heart will open, awaken, and you will merge into your higher God/Source love multi-dimensionally. This is usually when you awaken into your higher spiritual purpose. As you continue to expand into your light self, you will start feeling and experiencing the gifts of your intentions and efforts.

It is impossible to put the new on top of the old. You must release the old to have more room to expand into your higher more conscious, loving self.

You will start seeing all emotional agreements as gifts. If you had not experienced the pain, emptiness, loneliness, etc. you probably would not be looking for ways to heal, to move beyond your stories. Your painful emotions were gifts that assisted you to search for love. As you start seeing all of your life's experiences through the mirror of gifts, you will shift into a higher frequency of knowing. Your subconscious will open its files to the many memories and gifts of love from all time frames.

You will start seeing, feeling, and experiencing life from your heart, from love.

You may have a euphoric feeling as your body and consciousness awakens to the gift of love.

When your intention is to see and experience all life from the gift consciousness, you will bring so many amazing gifts into your life. More conscious people, places, and circumstances will instantly mirror their light and gifts for you. As you think it in thought, it will magically appear. You are morphing from the caterpillar into the beautiful butterfly of freedom.

The gift for me in writing this book has been the expansion

of my own self love. The Creator and my spiritual team have taken me through many emotional veils to the core of my karmic stories and agreements. I have released old, frozen emotional memories that were the glue holding my patterns together.

Every day with the continual love, support, and acceptance from the Creator and my spiritual team, I continue to awaken and expand into the higher vibrations of my own love. Many days I awake feeling a light dance of love and joy within myself. The dance starts from my root and spirals up through my chakras and my spine opening crystal light frequencies that fill my whole body and Being with joy, love, happiness, and grace.

I am so grateful to have come to this place of love in my life and for having such a strong, loving, supportive, compassionate, and hysterically humorous spiritual team. I am grateful to have the opportunity to assist you to open your heart to love and that your own divine essence will awaken your bodies and systems into the memories, safety, and dance of love.

If your intention is to live a spiritual life of love, joy, compassion, health, abundance, and freedom, etc. these simple tools will very quickly shift you into the morphogenetic field of these gifts. It is important to see and feel the emotional releases as gifts that bring you closer to your own heart's divine love.

It is your birthright and Soul's agreement in this lifetime to awaken into love and grace. I tell my story so that you will have hope and continue to persevere. This is the lifetime we have agreed to come full circle. Every painful, emotional experience you have gone through has a past frame of reference. It is an illusion. Love is the only truth there is. As you continue to live in the now and your intention is to release old programs, emotions, and stories, your now moment will become one of love, grace, happiness, joy, bliss, and freedom.

If I can do this, you can, too. You are not alone. You have many beautiful Beings of light (your spiritual team) that are holding your hand and walking with you as they guide you home into your own self love. The spiritual doors within you are wide open waiting for you to walk through into the center of your heart's divine essence of love. This is what we have waited for, to come home inside of ourselves to remember that we are love, and now the process to get there is simple. The gift of going through the release of the past is the expansion and awakening of your own joy and love. This joyous freedom awaits you to experience in the moment of now. Ask and you will receive!

The Creator – Opening My Heart to Divine Love

While working on the book, I awoke one morning in the divine presence of love. The light of love was filling my whole room with a crystal light frequency. As I lay there in bliss, the Creator showed me how to fill my body up with total love by using my own heart's divine/God presence. I could feel my own Source love spilling out of my heart like a fountain. This pure love energy filled my whole etheric body system with light. As the light continued to fill my DNA system, codings of light in the DNA were popping open and colors of crystal light were filling all of my body's systems with incredible love. I had moved into and merged with the morphogenetic field of Christ, Creator, I AM presence of love. As I lay there, I could not move, nor did I want to move. I was home in the heart of my own love. I was vibrating in my spark of divine love that I was created in. As I took this love into me, I could feel myself automatically taking deep breaths. God's breath was breathing me, breathing this love into every cell of my body and into all consciousness of my Being. I had found my way home and merged into another level of my Soul's love and grace.

The Creator then showed me how to send this pure love into my second chakra to release old karmic energies and contracts. As this fountain of love continued to flow into my second chakra, I could feel old stories and painful, frozen emotions melt and transmute out of form and into love. I could feel ripples of love moving through all dimensions, layers, and veils of my body, clearing out old emotional debris and filling me back up with love.

I felt like the old emotions were stones being thrown into the water, and ripples of love were expanding and clearing my bodies out like the ocean waves moving in and out of my systems. When the healing was complete, my whole body felt like a pristine, live river was running through it. I felt clean, pure, and in total harmony with all consciousness. I was in the home of love. Later in the book, I will take your through the process of the Creator teaching me how to teach you to open to your divine love.

Like attracts like, and as you vibrate in the beautiful rainbow colors and music of love, your life will become a multi-dimensional musical that expands and merges into the morphogenetic field of divine/God Source Love.

Your etheric DNA system will vibrate in oneness with Source.

Love is your truth, Source, and homecoming.

Welcome home!

∞

When a Soul feels compassion for another person's journey, a great healing starts taking place within them; their lens of perception shifts into a higher understanding.

~ Message from the CREATOR ~

∞

CREATOR'S INTRODUCTION

Many different beliefs, agreements, time frames, and emotions are playing out on your planet now. As you are ascending, your collective agreement is for all Beings and all consciousness to expand beyond timeframes and blend together beyond past, present, future. Your beginning memories and vibrations of love are like a river running through your bodies and cleaning out old, emotional debris of thought forms, belief systems, patterns, and perceptions.

As the river runs through you, it is moving you into your future self that carries within you great love, joy, wisdom, knowledge, and knowingness. You are coming full circle, home again within yourself into your divine essence of Me, of Creation. As your DNA is matching My DNA, memories of your own love, magnificence, inner power, and purpose are being activated.

We are one consciousness. In matching the DNA, you are moving beyond any so-called predisposed, genetic conditioning and re-awakening into your God/Creator Self. You are moving beyond karmic agreements and contracts and back into the heart and soul of love.

All genetic components are karmic, and when you are vibrating beyond karmic agreements, contracts, and emotional patterns, your body and whole Being will vibrate in love – the home and heart of all of Creation. In this vibration sickness and dis-ease cannot exist.

Scientists are now giving the name epigenetic to cells of Creation that have been vibrating in like consciousness since the beginning of time. I am your Creation; we have always been one consciousness. This is not new; it is just being remembered. As you are ascending, the veils of karma are lifting, and many memories of great knowledge and wisdom are re-awakening.

You would not be alive in your physical body today if your cells were not vibrating from a higher presence. You are the Cells of Me, a higher body of consciousness. This frequency of Me - your Father/Mother - is your Soul's genetic make-up and programming. Without Me, you would not be. You are Me. Your DNA is and has always been My DNA. You are now waking up and remembering your birthright of light's love. You have always vibrated above your earthly DNA. You are Spirit, the light of Love, in a physical body. Your DNA's home has always been above your earthly home.

So My beautiful Beings of light, your DNA has always been My DNA. It has been the thread of life that has kept you going through all of your lifetimes and Soul's agreements. You are just now waking up and remembering. You are coming home as me, as one consciousness inside of yourself.

When you were in a karmic time frame of fear through karmic religions, governments, control, and many other fearful beliefs and modalities, many of you Beings were matching the vibration of the intention of this control. Your DNA immediately followed the orders of the intentions, matched it, and merged with the morphogenetic field of fear.

Through the Ascension process that is happening now, many of you Master Souls are awakening and merging into your higher selves and into the consciousness of Me, your Creation. Your will and My will are blending together as one higher purpose. As you are merging, awakening and remembering that you are Masters and Co-Creators, your collective DNA is breaking the chain of history that has controlled so many through fear.

As you are vibrating in a higher consciousness, your lens of perception is shifting and many of you are experiencing and seeing the collective DNA or epigenetic field around the DNA responding to environmental frequencies.

These environmental matches have always been but could not be seen because the collective consciousness was matching the intention of fear, of control. The collective DNA's match was too dense to experience the high vibrational light that you are now experiencing.

As many of you are waking up to your own self-love and Mastery, you are opening portals of light for many others to awaken. These portals of light carry prisms of color and sound that shifts others' DNA into matching and merging with the collective ascension. This is creating an amazing awakening, or shift, in the collective consciousness. In reality what is happening is that your DNA is unraveling from collective fear and awakening, matching, and merging with the DNA of your

Soul's higher creation, with your divine spark of light, which is all-encompassing and inclusive love.

This love is your beginning and your end. You are a Being of light that is coming full circle back into your beginning birth of love. You are coming home inside of yourself. You are remembering. Your roots are love and from this remembering you have the choice to choose which frequency you desire to live your life from.

Because you are one collective consciousness that has split into many lessons, contracts and agreements, when your intention is to live from love, your collective DNA will turn on the love frequency for many other Souls to come home inside of themselves, to awaken, match, and merge with the higher vibration and Knowing of love.

Your collective DNA has always matched its environment, and now that you are awakening, through intention you can choose what vibration and morphogenetic field you want to match and merge with. You can choose to take an easier road of love that will awaken your own self-love and magnificence and match the collective I AM morphogenetic field of love or take a detour and continue to match all of your old, past hurts and fears. Before re-incarnating, you, with Spirit, chose your Soul's journey and the lessons that you needed to learn from, to move you through fear and into love. After you were born, you forgot your agreements. You needed to forget to remember. Your agreement was and is to move through the emotions of the lessons and agreements, to merge with your higher Self and into your OverSoul's higher consciousness system and blend together multi-dimensionally into **ONE** Soul's higher color/sound frequency.

As a Creator Being, your agreement is to choose your path as a Master Co-Creator and match and merge your DNA with the morphogenetic field of your choices.

As you vibrate in the higher sound frequencies of love, your love will ripple through the DNA system of other Creator Beings and assist them to awaken and remember their birthright of love.

My intention for this book is to assist you great Creator Beings that are My spark of light and love to easily shift out of duality and back home into **one love, one light,** and **one heart!** Your Soul's journey on the Earth has taken you through every story, belief system, emotion, religion, ethnic background, and color that has ever lived or vibrated on the Earth.

Your agreement now is to activate and draw from your Soul's innernet system your vast knowledge and wisdom and remember that you are the love, light, safety, compassion and freedom that can and will shift your world. You are the Master and Guru that you have waited for.

When the 2012 doorway opened, you moved beyond karmic contracts and agreements into the light and magnificence of your multi-dimensional Being. Your powerful light activated old emotional stories that were vibrating in the morphogenetic field of the contracts. Many of you felt foggy and confused like there was a tug-of-war between your own light and love.

From this fear and imbalance, you continued to look for ways to heal, to shift yourself out of duality and back into the heart of love.

The techniques in this manuscript will assist you to easily shift your etheric DNA system out of old, frozen emotions and into your own God Source, love, light, health, prosperity, and abundance on all levels. Your new contract and agreement is to awaken your Soul's higher purpose and live as the Master and Co-Creator of your life and destiny. The techniques will assist you to realign with the heart and mind of Me. You will merge with My unlimited Source energy that is so lovingly awaiting to assist in whatever your desires and intentions are. I am honored that I can assist you to consciously remember your own birthright, your own spark of divinity and that we can now vibrate home together as **one love.**

I love you, honor you, and thank you for your agreement to come to the Earth during the tremendous shift of conscious awakening. You are a Great Master teacher, and your light will shine upon many to assist them to remember their own light and divinity so that all can awaken into **one heart** of love.

∞

CHAPTER 1

THE CREATOR - WHAT IS DNA?

DNA is your Soul's history, or story, from the beginning of your spark of light, of creation. Some of you were created before My heart opened to the love of My Feminine Sophia. This is the collective DNA playing itself out in countries that do not honor the feminine.

Before you became a Soul, you were a collective thought form of My highest consciousness. When My heart opened, We – Sophia and I – created a balanced collective frequency of love, light, and compassion.

You, the Cells of this higher DNA frequency, are the wayshowers who are remembering who you are and are awakening into your magnificence. You are moving beyond karmic lessons and patterns and blending yourself multi-dimensionally into the collective DNA of Ascension and Enlightenment. You are the wings of freedom for all.

You have had many great Masters come to your planet and open the door to the light, to awaken love in all, and to assist to lighten the frequency for the Ascension.

Many of you are having spontaneous enlightenments and remembering. Through the Ascension, your collective DNA has shifted and is vibrating in the Master DNA. Your DNA has matched and merged into the morphogenetic field of the Master God/self DNA. Collectively you are assisting many to awaken, remember, and come home inside of themselves.

You, the Souls, or Cells of the Earth, are playing out different patterns, or programs of the DNA, and yet, collectively, you are one Soul/Cell of higher consciousness, because all is Me.

Many of the Souls in what you call third world countries are still living and acting out the patterns in the DNA of the Souls (Cells) that were created before My heart opened. They are at war against the feminine, against Me, My feminine.

After My heart opened and expanded, My love rippled into them, and they started experiencing feelings that they did not want to feel. They were used to experiencing themselves through the mind, not feelings. When this happened, they started rebelling against Me, the Father and against the feminine, My heart, Mother Sophia. They actually wanted Me to choose between them and My feminine heart. They were not willing to expand themselves into balance of the heart and mind or what you call the Male and the Female. Many of these Souls have reincarnated back to the Earth to play these old imbalances out and are warring against themselves.

They are actually warring against their own heart, their own feelings of love. Remember, you - we - are each other, and the feminine activates feelings that the male ego does not want to experience. All Souls that incarnated into that theme, or story, have agreed to do so, including the women, or feminine. It is in their collective DNA to shift through the imbalance to bring the feminine back into balance.

You also have those of you who are vibrating in your higher selves' collective DNA system and from Mother/Father/Creator's DNA. Your collective intention is to live from the Christ, I AM, Bodhisattva vibration of love, peace, forgiveness, thankfulness, and Oneness. Many of you are from the future and have agreed to lower your vibration, to come down to the Earth and hold the light for the karmic collective DNA to unravel, release, and move through the agreed upon assignment into completion.

All Beings on your Planet have all strands of DNA within them. The Beings that have agreed to play out the opposition have not completed their old assignments of fear. They are vibrating in the collective DNA of fear, of Ego, and your agreement is to hold the love and light for them to move into their higher love and Knowing. Your light is activating the collective God/Creator DNA systems. As they shift from fear to love, they open the door for many to remember their own love.

In our first book, *The Creator Speaks*, I spoke of the Earth being a hologram where all end times played themselves out. This is still happening now.

The Earth is a great Creator Being, or body of consciousness, whose purpose has been a learning program of death and rebirth.

The Earth is a hologram where Beings from all of my Planets and Creations love to come to learn lessons of Souls Awakening, individually and collectively. You have had many civilizations on your Planet. Some have died out, completing the karmic learning experience and others just left because their contracts were up.

All of these lessons, agreements, and contracts are in the DNA. As the karmic completion occurred, the DNA actually shifted out of the lesson and into the light or into the next level or lesson of the Soul's journey.

Although the DNA shifted, the memory or emotions of the experience are still in your DNA. This is what scientists call junk DNA; it is actually karmic DNA. Many times this DNA is not activated until you meet someone of like frequency or go through a similar emotion or pattern in this lifetime.

Your body and mind are live computer systems. As your emotion triggers or activates the DNA, the subconscious Googles up similar memories to bring the experience to the surface to be healed: sometimes through the actual emotions of the experience or through the body becoming overloaded and short circuiting with sickness and disease. Many times this is your Soul's wake-up call and agreement. Your agreement is to remember that you are a Master and Co-creator and that you can choose what frequency you desire to live life from. You can choose to consciously match and merge into the morphogenetic field of your higher intentions of love for yourself and the world. Love's frequency not only heals you but starts shifting the consciousness of the whole world. Because you all live from one cell consciousness of Me, your light and love starts rippling through the collective DNA system turning the light on in others. This creates a combustion of light that moves through, breaks open, and dissipates old, karmic sound frequencies of fear.

Every country has its own collective DNA where the consciousness of that DNA is being played out.

Each religion has its collective DNA that is being played out. Each race has its collective DNA being played out.

Many of you see and experience the Earth and its people in despair and hopelessness.

I see the Earth and its people in great hope, love, harmony, and freedom.

I see races of people that have moved beyond color and are marrying, or coming together with other races and creating new blended races of people.

I see the DNA of religions opening and blending with other religions, blending beyond creed and beliefs and opening their hearts to receive others and activating higher consciousness DNA.

I see religions that are accepting and loving gays, allowing all people to love one another regardless of color, gender, or religious beliefs. This is moving beyond karmic DNA.

I see people in oppressed countries who are fighting for freedom and who have moved beyond the fear of death. This activates a higher DNA consciousness for the people of the country. There is no death, just a death of old belief systems, karmic agreements and contracts, and a rebirth of a new lifetime.

I see children being born who are incarnating with the Christ, I AM DNA wide open. I see children who are being born so conscious that those around them must pay attention. The DNA of these children is activating the collective DNA of those around them, and those around them are waking up through the love of these children. I see these conscious, crystal children as the future of your world.

I see dark clouds of old DNA popping open and rainbows of light spilling and spewing out.

I see a world that is coming together and supporting each other with the highest intention for all.

I see a world that wants everyone to be safe and for all to have enough to eat.

I see a world whose collective DNA is blending together creating a symphony of sound so beautiful and loud with all notes of the scale - a song that is blasting away old karmic DNA.

I see a world whose music is so beautiful that it creates rainbows of color that assists to shift all realities and consciousness.

I see a world that blends together as **ONE**, as **one heart,** as **one love,** and awakens the collective DNA of my and Sophia's heart.

I see a world where all is my heart and love of my highest Creation.

I see a world where my DNA and yours blend together where there is no time, distance, or separation.

I see a world where my love and your love have created a DNA consciousness that is beyond any story.

I see a world that is awakening into its full bloom of higher knowing where Beings from all Planets and Creations have come together on this great Planet Earth to learn to blend all frequencies of Creation together as one symphony of Color and Sound of Creator DNA.

My intention is for all of you conscious Master Co-Creators to match and merge into the morphogenetic field of My truth for your world. As We merge together, We will create a symphony of color and sound so beautiful that all of the karmic Souls/ Cells of your world will awaken into their own magnificence and love. Our music will blend with their inner music and shift the world through karmic veils and back into My heart, your heart, Our **one heart** and home of love.

I love you. I am you. We are one consciousness. You are a spark of My Divine light, the stars of My Creation that have agreed to hold the light for many others to awaken: the domino effect. As We merge together as one light, We will fill the skies and your world with rainbows of color so beautiful that all hearts will remember their birthright of love. Merge with My intention for all, for We are one – I love you.

Mother, Father, Creator

∞

CHAPTER 2

MICHELLE'S STORY

I started working with healing the DNA in 2007 after I was diagnosed with cancer.

I received my cancer diagnosis a week before I was leaving for a three month working tour to Sweden.

I decided to go on the tour anyway with the intention to heal myself. I remember thinking, "I am a healer; I'm going to heal myself." With that intention, I started looking at who else in my family had experienced similar health issues to mine. I could see that it was my Dad, and the intuitive thought came to me to travel into his DNA.

My spiritual team guided me to travel etherically through my father's DNA. My whole life's journey or goal has been to heal myself and my family. I did not want to raise my family with the patterns I was raised with but did not know how to do it differently. My quest has always been to unravel and heal the old emotional hurts, beliefs, patterns and stories. I was amazed that while journeying through my father's DNA, I could actually see and feel many of the patterns that for many years I had been working on clearing. They were very strong emotionally, like neon lights. We have heard, or experienced, that we marry our fathers and mothers. We become an extension of their energy patterns and play them out by bringing people and circumstances into our lives to mirror our patterns back to us. Although I knew this, I was totally shocked to actually see and feel the patterns. I was amazed to experience them unraveling from me. It felt like thread being pulled out of my etheric body. I thought, "Oh my God, I really have married my Father and all of my relationships with men really were aspects of my Father's energy, programming, and patterns."

While in my father's DNA, I could actually see, feel, and experience many of the patterns that were handed down through him from my ancestors.

My father had become an extension of the patterns, and I could see that I had agreed for them to be handed down to me to play out and release.

With my spiritual team, I started breaking my energy loose from the DNA patterns and emotional systems, and through Soul retrieval, I was able to bring back into me, my light, health, energy, and life force that had been trapped in the patterns.

As I mentioned, I could see and experience how my DNA patterns from my father had played out in my life bringing my father back to me not only in relationships with men but also in many other aspects of my life.

Around the time that I had discovered I was an extension of my father's and ancestral DNA patterns, I saw a cancer specialist in Sweden who informed me that my cancer had spread and that I should to go back to Hawaii (where I was living) and take care of myself.

When I received this diagnosis, I felt myself immediately fill with fear and go into a frequency of death ... a death sentence. I realized that I had moved into cancer's morphogenetic field, which for many has been death. At that time I did not know that my collective DNA had matched the cancer death sentence.

I thought, "This is not me. I don't think like this," and I started breaking myself loose from the collective fear frequency of cancer by surrendering into the center of it. I would connect myself multi-dimensionally with my spiritual team, with all of their love, light, and colors and through our collective intention, I would blast myself into the center of the death field breaking it loose from my body. As soon as I released my etheric body from the morphogenetic death field, I could see my etheric body fill up with prisms of rainbow light.

After I released my body from the morphogenetic field of cancer's death, my thoughts also changed. I no longer felt fear of death, of death by cancer. I felt hope, joy, and a re-birth of freedom. I knew that I was going to heal and make it through my cancer experience.

My intention was to continue to heal myself by traveling into and through my father's DNA. This process was so powerful that I decided to go into my mother's ancestor's DNA to break old, fear-based, emotional patterns of fear, guilt, shame, loneliness, depression, hopelessness, life's hardships, of not being good enough, sickness, dis-ease, etc. and anything else I could think of. Once again through Soul retrieval, I brought back into me, my life force energy that had been trapped in the patterns.

I decided to go back to Hawaii and have the cancer surgery because I had a very busy touring schedule and wanted to quickly move on with my life and was not sure how much time I would need to heal the cancer without the surgery. **I received one of the greatest gifts of my life – "My Life!"**

When I went in for my surgery, not a trace of cancer was found. I knew that my DNA healing had broken genetic, ancestral systems, and karmic patterns. I had cleared myself beyond the emotions of the story, of the dis-ease. Through Soul retrieval I had brought my light, love, health and life force energy back into me.

Because the healing had been so profound, I decided to continue to travel through my parents' ancestral DNA releasing old emotional programs and patterns. From this continual cycle of release I was amazed that I started to see and feel light running through my DNA. This light crystal energy ran from my DNA through my parents and ancestors DNA systems and back into my spiritual bloodline, or tribe. I experienced myself with the Masters and Angels, vibrating in Jesus, Magdalene Christ energy as I moved and merged into the Creator's heart of love and in the Isness before time. I could feel my Cells like crystals, prisms of rainbow color waking up and tingling with love, light, and joy – freedom. All levels of my body felt like they had come home and were blending together in a beautiful symphony of color and sound. Once again, I was in the heart and flow of love.

This experience was proof that we can heal and change our

DNA; in doing so we heal ourselves and break the patterns of sickness/dis-ease for our ancestral lineage backwards and forward.

As we clear out old, karmic systems, patterns, and agreements, our light Creator DNA is activated. This shifts us and our ancestors collectively into light, love, and magnificence multi-dimensionally.

We come home together beyond duality.

Since that time and incredible healing experience, I have brought the DNA healing modality into my workshops. From DNA healing and Soul retrieval, I have witnessed so many miraculous healings for others. It is pretty amazing what people will find and experience in their parent's ancestral DNA system.

A woman in one of my workshops was traveling through her mother's DNA and actually met her mother who had died many years before. Her mother was able to come through the opened DNA and communicate with the woman. The woman could feel her mother's love and how proud she was of her. Her mother's love allowed her to feel safe enough to let go of so much of her frozen, emotional pain. The woman sobbed as her mother assisted her to continue her journey through the DNA releasing old programs and misconceptions.

Her mother had died when she was a child, which left her with the feelings of abandonment, guilt, of not being wanted and of not being good enough. She had continued to match these patterns of DNA by bringing others into her life that would invalidate, dishonor, and abandon her just like her mother did.

From the DNA healing with her mother, she felt loved, wanted, valued, safe, and empowered. Her inner children felt like they were in the heart, warmth, and love of their mother, which they were. She was able to break the patterns and to set healthy boundaries for herself and bring people into her life who matched her higher vibrational DNA and who also valued and loved her.

Your shadow patterns are also in the DNA. Both parents of a man in one of my workshops had been in Auschwitz, Poland during WWII. His father had lost his wife and son in the camp. His parents were brought to Sweden and met in Sweden after the war.

This man had a very challenging life and when he traveled into his father's DNA, he was terrified. He felt a dark force chasing him. He felt like he was in a nightmare and couldn't wake up or come out of it. He was in the morphogenetic field of the dark Shadow of war and death. This fear frequency had been vibrating through him creating conflict and struggle his whole life. He had lived much of his life from this terror and death frequency but because his Soul's higher purpose and agreement was so strong, his light was able to pull him through the collective, dark death experiences.

While in the DNA, Spirit assisted him to cut the Shadow dark force cords of fear and through Soul retrieval bring his light, safety, love, and life force back into him.

His second journey through the ancestral DNA was much lighter. He had broken and released many of the dark Shadow patterns for himself and his ancestors.

The more you go into and clear DNA patterns, the easier your life becomes. After you clear the patterns, it is important to go up through the Pineal Gland in the center of your brain into your God/Creator DNA and set new intentions for this new lifetime that we are now awakening and merging into. You are re-programming your conscious and subconscious minds and are re-aligning yourself with the super conscious mind of God, of Creation. This alignment will download the higher color/sound frequency of your intentions into your Cells activating and shifting your DNA into the collective consciousness of the intention.

Because like attracts like, you will match, merge, and bring a more harmonious energy back to you. You will start experiencing all walks of life from the morphogenetic field of Source, as a Co-Creator of Choice, of Love, of Freedom, of Oneness.

Your lens of perception will be from the Heart, Love, Mind and Will of God.

At the same time I started sharing the DNA healing technique in my workshops, a spiritual team of Crystal Light Beings showed up and started working with the etheric bodies of the attendees.

They identified themselves as Crystal Creator Beings that work directly with the Creator.

I was shown that the etheric body has a collective DNA system and from that day forward this team have always been my assistants, both in workshops and my private sessions.

In all of my sessions and workshops, my Crystal team always clears the client's and attendee's etheric body's collective DNA system. Although I have seen and experienced this clearing and healing for many years, I had never actually seen inside of the collective DNA system.

I have experienced the Crystal Creator Beings, clearing energy from the collective DNA system by pulling out programs, patterns, implants, microchips, and even curses.

I actually see the room filling with these Beings of Light who start clearing out the etheric body. They do this so we can see and experience clearly any imbalances in the different levels of the physical body. I always feel so blessed and honored to be part of such an incredibly powerful, healing team.

In one of my workshops, a woman was in so much pain that she could hardly function. She actually wanted to leave the workshop. I felt so much love and compassion for her and asked her to please stay. I felt that we (Spirit and I) would be able to clear her body out. I could feel that the situation she was in was pretty serious. Because I was facilitating the group, I was not able to give her the amount of individual time or attention that I could see she needed. I asked Spirit to assist, which they always do, but this was on another level. While facilitating a spiritual process for the group, I looked over and saw a man with long, white hair and a long, white beard standing in front of her. I realized it was Melchizedek. I was surprised but also excited to see him so clearly. I felt a great love, light, amazement, and magical joy within myself.

After the Crystal Creator Beings had cleared the collective DNA system of the group, Melchizedek had physically manifested and was standing in front of the woman. He had a crystal light body and a very strong, broad, powerful presence that filled the room with light. I watched Melchizedek pull an implant out of the woman's heart. He then turned around and winked at me. Although my team always assists, I don't usually see them physically manifest so clearly in the room. I usually see them more etherically. I felt Melchizedek knew the seriousness of her situation and was making a point to show me they are always assisting me and us. We are never alone.

I felt his powerful intentional force and also his humor, love, light, and magic and a knowing that we are on the same team, working for the same purpose: to assist the Planet to heal by assisting Souls to shift beyond all stories, out of old karmic energies and contracts, and into Ascension, Enlightenment, and Oneness.

After the process was over, I asked the woman how she felt, and of course she responded with a very broad smile and said, "Just great!" I said, "On the break I will tell you what happened." She was elated and for the rest of the workshop the physical pain and mental fuzziness was gone. She was laughing with others and was full of joy and happiness, and she experienced a sense of love and expansive freedom. After the workshop she was still experiencing overwhelming love, health, freedom, and joy.

The collective DNA system is connected to the collective consciousness of the world, and vibrates in the morphogenetic field of whatever the person's beliefs or perceptions are. Many times the subconscious mind is holding the collective DNA hostage because the person is still vibrating in and holding programs from past lives, earlier childhood experiences, and other traumatic life experiences and memories. It may be difficult for the person to move forward because the person's emotions are frozen from the earlier trauma and they are still vibrating collectively in the fear, or shock, of the experience. PTSS: Post traumatic stress syndrome may also be from other lifetimes or past life experiences.

Until we become aware and conscious enough to break the patterns, we continue to play them out. Our etheric body's DNA system vibrates in the morphogenetic field and reinforces the patterns and because like-attracts-like, you continue to draw like consciousness back to you.

When your intention is to clear and move out of the old karmic emotional patterns, programs, and systems, your spiritual team will step in and connect you with the people that can assist you in your healing process. All you have to do is ask and you will receive. Spirit is very willing to assist in whatever way you may need their assistance. They are waiting for you to ask.

At first you may think it is a coincidence that you have met someone that has the exact tools that you need at that time to help you or assist you.

As you continue your journey through and into your Soul's Awakening, you will know that there are no coincidences, that each step of the way you were and are divinely guided and directed. By this time of your Soul's awakening, you may have become aware of or even connected to many of the spiritual guides and teachers from other dimensions that have been assisting you.

In every level of your awakening, or unraveling, your collective DNA was always matching and merging with the frequency of your awakened wisdom. This merge actually gave you the strength to persevere. Your whole collective team of like consciousness (both in Spirit and on Earth) held the frequencies for you to shift your DNA into the higher knowing or octaves of yourself multi-dimensionally. Your etheric DNA system matched and merged with your collective spiritual team's and held the strength, love, and light for you to move beyond karma and into the super conscious mind of Love, of God, of Creator.

As you awaken, your collective DNA system will vibrate in the strength of the super consciousness and your unwavering strength will hold the light to assist others to match and merge with the collective God/Creator/Source DNA of Oneness.

As I explained, I have worked with healing and shifting the physical DNA for many years and the Crystal Creator Beings have assisted me by healing and clearing the etheric DNA systems ... but I had never seen inside of the etheric DNA system until last year (2014) while on a tour in Sweden.

After an experience (that will be explained in the next chapter) the Creator opened the etheric DNA system of a client and showed me how it works and what its purpose and intention is. Our bodies, these live computer systems, are really amazing Creator Beings, and I am honored to share the knowledge and the techniques that the Creator brought through me to give to you. And the gift is that these techniques and processes are so simple and easy to do. We have collectively worked so hard to heal and love ourselves and the Creator is honoring us by bringing easy processes to assist us to move very quickly into self love, into the true Master and Co-Creator within ourselves, to become **one love, one light.**

∞

"Absolutely everything, all consciousness, is color and sound, and when you become conscious of this you can choose which color sound frequencies you desire to vibrate in. Remember, like attracts like."

~ Message from the CREATOR ~

∞

CHAPTER 3

THE COLLECTIVE DNA'S MATCH AND MERGE (THE CREATOR TEACHING ME)

While on a three-month tour in Sweden, I had an amazing experience of the Creator opening up the collective DNA of a client to show me how our collective DNA system works, what it looks like, and how it functions.

I was seeing clients and facilitating a workshop in Sweden and was around a person who was going through a "Dark Night of the Soul" similar to what I had gone through many years ago. As she continued to talk about it, I could feel the frequency start to come in to me. I could feel my etheric body opening up to the vibration. I am usually pretty good at blocking energies, but I was not able to block the frequency.

As my etheric (energy) body was taking in the frequency, I could actually feel my subconscious opening up to a previous experience that I had gone through. I felt a fear; a fear of opening up, and going through a similar "Dark Night of the Soul" nightmare experience again.

That night, I had an exhaustion that I could not seem to shake off. When I awoke the following day, I just thought, "This is crazy." I went up through my Pineal Gland (in the center of my brain), my DNA connection to Source –to Mother/Father/Creator - and disconnected from the collective fear frequencies of the Shadow patterns that had created the exhaustion. I then felt great, free, and happy and excited about life again; I felt like myself.

That day while working with my first client, the Creator showed me how the collective DNA opens up and is always matching whatever vibration it is around. I was shown how my collective DNA had matched and merged with the other woman's "Dark Night of the Soul" experience. I was experiencing the match while it was happening but thought I was just taking her energy into me. I could feel her energy coming into my etheric body and was not able to block it because unknown to me my collective DNA was matching and merging with hers. My subconscious mind had opened up to my similar Shadow experiences, and my fearful emotions matched hers. I knew how easy it is to take in other people's energy but did not understand the DNA match until the Creator opened up the collective DNA of my client. I could literally see the collective DNA (in the etheric body of the woman I was assisting) open up, match, and merge with her higher self.

I could see thousands of little tentacles, or strands of DNA, unraveling throughout her whole, etheric energy body. They were waving magically and freely like the wind. The best way I can describe it is the tentacles or DNA strands were all waiting to be fed energy.

As I witnessed them opening up, I saw many beautiful rainbow colors of light spiraling open, taking in and absorbing all of the energy around them; they were absorbing their environment.

As soon as the collective DNA matches its surrounding environment, the frequencies merge together and the person's bodies and systems activate similar memories from what we call past experiences or time frames. If the match is negative or fear-based, the physical DNA will respond to the emotions of the experience sending the fear frequency through the body.

If the match is a high vibrational light energy, the physical DNA will shift into the higher vibration and send the frequency through the whole body, many times activating codings in the DNA. The person may wake up and remember their higher purpose and agreements on the Earth and shift multidimensionally into their light body selves.

As I was watching the Creator show me this incredible light show experience, I could actually feel my collective DNA matching the higher vibration of the Creator's DNA. My body felt like thousands of crystal butterflies, or Angel wings, flowing and swaying in the energy of love. These strands of my DNA were opening up and being fed by Creation.

As my collective DNA matched the Creator's, I could feel my whole body fill with beautiful colors and prisms of light and sound. I became a musical of love within myself.

I then moved into the center of this experience and felt my whole body and Being resonate in an incredible silence.

In the center of the silence was a peace and knowing that absolutely all is in Divine Order and that all is playing out just as it should be.

The client and I were both very excited to experience this. We then matched her connection to Source/I AM Creator and through our excitement matched anything else we could think of. The experience was profound. I felt beautiful, crystal rainbows of light dancing within me. What is interesting is that morning she had asked Spirit to teach her more about the DNA.

Ask and you shall receive.

Since that time I have not felt that overwhelming tiredness or exhaustion. Before working with clients, I make sure I match and merge my DNA with my higher self, Mother/Father I AM energy, my spiritual team, and the higher self of the client.

I was shown how the DNA opens, matches, and merges with whatever vibration it is around. It matches the environment. The Creator said our collective DNA is always, always matching from the time we are first born. At birth, we still have such a strong connection to Spirit and our collective DNA system is still merged with our higher self – Mother/Father/God/Angelic DNA. When we get to the age of about two years old, our collective DNA starts matching our environment. Until then we are still very much awake and in the flow of Spirit.

At conception, we begin downloading our karmic genetic patterns. By the time we are born into this lifetime, we have already programmed our whole emotional genetic story that we have agreed to play out.

If we immediately began playing out our patterns upon our birth, the earthly vibration would be too different and dense from our existing light frequency, and we would have an electrical blowout. Our nervous system would not be able to survive the difference in frequencies.

Until about the age of two, we are still gliding on the wings of Spirit and vibrating in the morphogenetic field of Source Love. When children grow to about the age of two, they emerge more fully into the physical body. At that time many of the agreed upon karmic lessons and emotions start unraveling, and the child starts playing them out. This is what many call the terrible two's.

These emotions expand into the etheric body system, which is the home of the collective DNA. This collective DNA starts looking for a match of the feelings and emotions and starts matching and merging with the parents' DNA and the DNA of its environment. Anything in the collective DNA system immediately starts moving or shifting into the physical body. Until around two, the collective DNA is mostly matching the higher vibrational sound of Spirit.

Many of us have experienced being around someone, and all of a sudden, we feel sadness, grief, anger, or emotions that we were not feeling until we were in the person's energy.

Our collective DNA matched and merged with that person's emotional energy and we absorbed it into our physical body. Our subconscious then Googled up past memories within us of similar emotions, which strengthened the match. As we become more aware and realize that we have picked up energies that are not ours, we can release them by choosing to match a more harmonious frequency. Until then, we may play out the absorbed, emotional match of others and create more conflict in our lives that does not necessarily have to be our story to play out.

You may also be around someone who is happy and joyful and will experience your mood shift. You will feel lighter, happier, more joyful and connected. Again, your subconscious assisted by Googling up similar experiences where you were happier and more joyful. This strengthened the match. Our collective DNA is always matching, and whatever it matches we absorb and become a part of.

If a child is matching conflict, fear, insecurities, not being safe, not feeling loved, etc., this energy enters the child's body and the subconscious will look into its file system and download similar emotional memories, creating a sense of not being valuable, wanted, important, or safe, of not being worthy enough to be loved. The energy creates a feeling of mistrust and a lack of a self-worth. The child may continue to play out this energy bringing people and circumstances back to himself to mirror the emotional pattern. The belief may play out into adulthood or until an awareness that a healing needs to take place. If a conscious understanding and healing of these emotions does not take place, the emotions end up frozen and may come out in anger, rage, disrespect, and many times the need to hurt others (the way the person has been hurt) allowing a release of the pent-up, confused, fear-based emotions.

If the child-adult-person is vibrating in these lower

emotional sound frequencies, the collective DNA will search for and draw others of like frequencies to mirror, match and merge with – birds of a feather flock together.

This is why people of low self-esteem search for others of like energy. With the subconscious assistance, the collective DNA matches and merges with this vibration as its truth. This person usually does not feel comfortable with others of a higher light sound frequency. The higher light/sound frequency may actually activate the fear-based emotions in the person. As the collective DNA matches fear-based emotions, it will search for and bring back to itself, from others, the same sound- and color frequencies. It then feels fed, and although it may be painful, the person feels comfortable in this energy.

If a child grows into adulthood with a sense of love, self-worth, support, and validation, he will most likely draw others into his life of validation and support. His collective DNA system is vibrating in the frequency of love and support multi-dimensionally. The subconscious will open up and download more love and support, and this person will draw like vibration back to himself.

Many times children from loving, supportive parents who have had great childhoods and may have been raised in God-based homes seem to go in the opposite direction. This is a karmic agreement that the child or person needed to understand, complete, or play out.

The parents' agreement has been to hold the love and light for this child or person to move through the journey with love and support. If this is the agreed upon journey together, it is important for the parent to continue to send love and match the child's DNA system with solid strength and support. Many times this means one has to let go of the outcome and let God and Spirit assist. At the same time, it is important to match and merge your heart and mind to the heart and mind of God-Creator-Love and as a Master and Co-Creator hold this vibration for all involved.

Absolutely everything, all consciousness, is color and sound, and when you become conscious of this you can choose which color sound frequencies you desire to vibrate in. Remember, like attracts like.

Many times a person of a higher light vibration, or frequencies, may enter the energy field of a person vibrating in a fear frequency. As this happens the light frequency may activate old, dormant emotions that the fear-based person does not want to feel.

Their collective DNA is matching and turning on memories in the person's DNA of the higher vibrational frequencies

The sound in the person's body may become confused; the light is activating old emotions and the tones of love and light merge with the tones of fear, conflict, and confusion. An emotional explosion happens. Many times this is the wake-up call that the person's Soul has asked for.

Anything in the etheric (energy) body that is not cleaned out enters the physical body. If a person is vibrating in fear-based emotions energetically, the etheric DNA with the assistance of the subconscious may activate the entire lineage of karmic, genetic, ancestral patterns in the physical DNA. Many times the awakened collective emotional patterns create sickness and disease in the physical body. Emotions affect and shift the DNA. From this sickness and dis-ease "wake-up call," the person receives the spiritual gift of looking for ways to heal and sometimes even live.

The same is true for a person whose intention is to awaken spiritually. As the collective DNA along with its partner, the subconscious, vibrates, matches, and merges with others who have awakened, or whose intention is to wake up, the collective DNA sends messages to the physical DNA. DNA codings may activate through the whole ancestral bloodline of awakened states of consciousness. Spiritual gifts, or modalities from other lifetimes, may be activated and the person's perception of life may change quickly, shifting them into a totally new experience of life. From the higher perception, their choices in life change. Many times they leave relationships and circumstances or change jobs that no longer fulfill them or match their new consciousness. They choose to live a more fulfilling life. They may shift into a broader consciousness with the intention of assisting others and the world to heal. They move out of the "I ME" Earthly karmic consciousness and into the collective "I AM" into the Master and Co-Creator within themselves.

The subconscious mind plays a big part of your Soul's journey through the DNA.

As your collective DNA is doing its job and constantly matching and merging with its environment, the subconscious will also match the emotional vibration of the body and mind's experience.

The subconscious is like Google. It will go into its vast memory, or file system, of all experiences that your Soul has ever agreed to go through and download them, or awaken them into your emotions and physical body. The subconscious brings all memories up at once because it cannot discern between past, present, and future. Imagine your body-mind as a live computer system, and as you move into an emotional pattern, your subconscious Googles up all inner websites, agreements, contracts, lifetimes, emotions, and patterns that are similar to what you are experiencing. There truly is no past, present, or future, but in third dimensional reality, we have lowered our consciousness into a time frame to be able to move through and release old beliefs, emotions, stories, and agreements. We have agreed to ascend beyond karma and into our multi-dimensional, higher selves and into **Oneness**. If we lived all experiences at once, we could not survive the vast multi-dimensional knowledge, experiences, and emotions that we carry within us. (We might end up in a mental institution – and some do.) We must have experiences in a time slot to be able to survive.

But ... your emotions do not vibrate in a timeline; they still vibrate multi-dimensionally in your physical body. They do not know the difference between past, present, and future. They feel like whatever is going on is in the now (which it is).

In matching another's DNA, your subconscious may have opened you up to other lifetimes of similar emotional patterns that created sickness and dis-ease. Your physical body then plays out the past memories as if they are happening now, and the accumulated energies become too toxic and difficult and the body once again closes down, short circuits; hence, sickness: dis-ease.

I believe this is the lifetime that we have agreed to come full circle, to move beyond emotional, karmic, ancestral patterns that create conflict, sickness, and dis-ease.

Anything in this lifetime has a frame of reference elsewhere. We have come into this lifetime to free ourselves from many of these old, karmic, genetic agreements and patterns.

We are ascending and moving beyond karmic time frames. As the collective ascension light is hitting our bodies and systems, our collective DNA is gratefully matching and responding by sending light waves into our physical DNA. The subconscious is Googling up other memories, or lifetimes, when we have ascended, when we have been great Masters and Teachers living from our Soul's higher purpose and doing great spiritual work. People are having great spontaneous awakenings. They are remembering and opening up to higher dimensions of themselves, dimensions where aspects of themselves walk and live as Masters-Teachers-Angels, where higher aspects of themselves are actually teaching them in this dimension. They are actually channeling and downloading higher Knowing frequencies of themselves.

Until the 2012 doorway, we were vibrating multi-dimensionally karmically, sometimes in a pretty low emotional color sound vibration. Because we are always matching and merging, we would bring more of the old worn-out story to us. As we shifted through the 2012 doorway collectively, we aligned and awakened into our light body selves multi-dimensionally. Our own light body activated old programs, emotions, and belief systems that no longer served us. We actually moved into a new lifetime without physically leaving the body. The new lifetime's chakra is the thymus; it is a beautiful aqua turquoise color. For many years, while doing healings on others, I could actually see a map of the person's karmic journey running through their whole body. It looked like an actual map with the dark lines moving through the meridians, organs, and whole system. I could see blockages in systems from old, karmic patterns and agreements.

Now when I look into people's bodies, I see the beautiful crystal aqua turquoise color filling in the old, dark, karmic lines. I experience their bodies flooding with the sounds of color, of newness, of rebirth. I can see and feel all levels of their bodies starting to harmonize with each other and vibrate with their higher selves' consciousness. Many times without me explaining or saying anything, the person I am working with will say to me, "I see my body filling with beautiful aqua-turquoise colors."

The new, higher color and love frequencies are creating havoc in many of our bodies' systems. The old, karmic glue is melting away. There is nothing holding the old us together. Our bodies are opening up to so many beautiful sounds, colors, and music. We are losing our old identities and beliefs. This is creating confusion in many and yet at the same time a freedom from old stories and beliefs.

I hear so many of you say, "I know I have a higher purpose. I need to find it. My old life is meaningless." Even though you don't quite understand or know what the new is, you are consciously choosing to let go of the old and move into a knowing that there is a new you. Through intention and matching your DNA with higher spiritual energy, you will merge into the morphogenetic field of the Creator's Source energy, and together Co-Create your new foundation and Soul's higher purpose on the Earth now.

∞

"Many scientists used to believe that the Pineal Gland was just a dormant gland hanging out in the center of your brain. Some of them now understand that the Pineal Gland is your DNA connection to Source"

~ Message from the MOTHER/FATHER/CREATOR ~

∞

CHAPTER 4

PINEAL GLAND'S DNA CONNECTION TO SOURCE

Many scientists used to believe that the Pineal Gland was just a dormant gland hanging out in the center of your brain. Some of them now understand that the Pineal Gland is your DNA connection to Source – Mother/Father/Creator. It is what opens and aligns your higher intelligence with the superconsciousness of Source. As the Source energy activates your DNA, it actually assists to connect and ground you to Mother Earth's higher self and purpose.

In my first book, *The Creator Speaks*, the Creator explains that in December 2012 when we moved through the 2012 doorway, Mother Earth actually shifted and merged together with her male aspect. His aspect is called Father Earth. Father Earth is not a physical Being. He is an etheric energy source that is assisting our beautiful Mother back into balance, into the heart of her Beloved male aspect.

Mother Earth has an agreement with the Source (Creator) to assist you and the collective consciousness to move out of duality and back into **one** Being of the I AM of All That Is. You are the links and live portals between Heaven and Earth that are assisting all of Creation and Gaia into Ascension.

As all consciousness is ascending, we are moving collectively into the balance of the Male and Female within ourselves and through all levels of Creation. This includes Mother Earth.

She is very content to be back in balance with her Beloved partner, Father Earth.

To make the link with Mother/Father Creator, it is important to open the Pineal Gland and ground the higher Source energy through you into Mother/Father Earth. The Pineal Gland in the center of the brain is your DNA connection to Source to your own divine, all knowing I AM presence.

Years ago, when the Creator showed me how to open people's Pineal Gland, I was amazed how beautiful this DNA is when it opens. I could literally see the DNA unfolding and reaching up through dimensions into the heart of Mother/ Father Creation. Although this gland is in the center of our brain, its real home is in the heart of Creation. When I started working with opening the Pineal Gland DNA, I was surprised at how much the DNA responds to energy, sounds, tones, music, and voice.

As I started opening and activating Pineal Glands, they seemed to know their way home. I could see these beautiful strands of colors in the center of the person's brain unwinding and opening into rainbows of color and prisms of light and into the heart of Love/God/Creation.

I was amazed at how different everyone's Pineal Glands were and yet very much the same.

Some Pineal Glands were like children and very excited to open up and show off their colors as they made their way home. Some were very wide and instantly opened into a portal of light as these magnificent strands of color unwound and moved into the heart of Creator. Others struggled because of old, unresolved, karmic agreements with God or Spirit. These glands did not feel safe to open up and move home into God/Source.

To open these Pineal Glands, I would move into my heart and from my loving I AM presence, my voice would reassure the gland that it was safe to open up and move home into the heart and love of God.

In all Pineal Glands' openings, I would connect my finger to the Pineal Gland of the person and move it up out of the top of their head. I felt so honored to be able to watch all of the beautiful colors open and unwind as they made their way home with God.

The Pineal Glands that were struggling with fear or mistrust would take longer. As I talked to them, I would keep them connected to my finger, and gently guide them home. Instead of a natural re-birth connection with the Source, it was more like a cesarean birth where I actually opened them and gently carried them home to the Source. I never experienced a gland not opening or making its way home into Source. Once the gland felt safe, it was elated to be home in the love, heart, and safety of Creation.

The Creator explains that everything is color and sound. It is pretty amazing to experience another person's DNA opening all of its rainbow colors as it responds to your heart and the sound of your voice. From this, one truly understands that we are one consciousness.

In smaller workshops, I (with Spirit) still open the attendees' Pineal Glands individually. When I am speaking or working with larger audiences, the room fills up with all variations of Spirit, and they assist to open the Pineal Glands of everyone in the room. It is pretty exhilarating for me to watch all of the beautiful glands magically open up to the Source and then witness streams of rainbow light coming back down through the crown chakra, through the center of the brain and filling their bodies up with so much light and love.

As the collective Pineal Gland activation takes place, the whole room fills with so many colorful light beams. All Beings in the room vibrate in a beautiful light show. Through the collective Pineal Gland opening, all Souls' higher selves merge together as one higher God/Self in human form. All blend together as one beyond any time frame.

It is very humbling to experience someone else's DNA opening up like a flower as it responds to the safety of my voice and heart, and if my energy and voice affect other people's Pineal Glands on this level, what does my voice and energy do to my own DNA?

As an experiment, imagine your body's DNA feeling all of its beautiful colors. Now talk to that DNA. (You don't even have to know what it is exactly; Your DNA knows itself.)

Tell the DNA that you love it. Thank it for being a great guiding light for you. Send love to it. As you talk to your DNA. Send love and laughter to it. Sing to it. Reassure it that it is now safe to open up to its light, love, joy, abundance, and health. Stay with this for a minute or so. How does your body feel?

I suggest that you do this process daily. It is so easy. It just takes a few seconds. You can do it while you are driving, in the shower, or any other place. Throughout the day, be conscious of what energy you are sending to your DNA. Your DNA will happily respond. Remember your DNA responds to your voice and to feelings and emotions. Your emotions shift your DNA. Send the intention of love to your DNA, and your etheric body's DNA will match it and merge with the morphogenetic field of love.

As you shift your body's DNA system with love, you are changing the molecules in your body. Dr. Masaru Emoto (The water master from Japan) experimented by putting different words on bottles of water. As he did this, it almost instantly completely changed the structure of the water.

Your bodies are mostly water – fluid – liquid. As you love, support, and thank your DNA, the love frequency will run through all of the liquid in your bodies bringing your body's systems into balance and harmony.

∞

CHAPTER 5

PINEAL GLAND ACTIVATION

With assistance from Spirit, you who are reading this and following the instructions of the technique will have your Pineal Gland activated.

The Creator has shared the Pineal Gland activation technique not only with me but with many others around the world. Our agreement is to assist with the collective Pineal Gland activation and open the collective DNA connection with Source to move us into ONE higher consciousness. The more of us who connect our DNA with the super consciousness of the Creator DNA, the easier it will be for us to collectively move through the multi-dimensional birth canal of Ascension and into Oneness.

We are the Cells of each other, and as we continue to collectively open our DNA to match, merge with, and live from the Creator's superconscious DNA, we are assisting the world to come home together as **one heart, one mind,** and **one love** of Creation.

We have agreed to awaken and shift individually into portals of light and merge together collectively to anchor with the Earth's (Gaia's) DNA systems to shift all consciousness into the higher dimensions of light multi-dimensionally.

We are the light carriers and the portals of light between Heaven and Earth. We are the I AM of All That Is. We truly are the ones that we have been waiting for. We are coming home, and our Pineal Gland DNA connection with the heart of Creation is the link to the heart of Mother Earth.

The Pineal Gland Process

Imagine bringing a Golden line of energy up from the center of your root chakra, into and through your second chakra (about two inches below the navel), through your solar plexus, heart, thymus, throat, and third eye chakra into the center of your brain where your Pineal Gland is positioned. Now move your golden line of energy up through your Pineal Gland out through your crown, as high up as you can imagine and into the heart of Love, of the Creator. Your Pineal Gland is waiting for your energy and intention to open it up, to move it home.

By doing this, you are actually moving a Golden Cord of light, or band, up through your chakras and into the 13th dimension, the home of Christ, the Masters, the Bodhisattva, and the Central Sun's Energy. This dimension is a major portal and system where all systems of the Creator energies connect and support each other. As your Pineal Gland opens up into this dimension, it merges multi-dimensionally with the heart, mind, and love of the Creator. Because we are one consciousness, as you merge with the Creator's light, an awakening of the Creator's intention of our world's highest purpose opens and awakens within you. Your DNA system opens and matches the higher mind of Creation and of your Soul's higher purpose. You don't have to know where this dimension is; just set your intention for your spiritual team to guide you, to move the Golden Cord of energy up through your chakras activating your Pineal Gland and moving it up through your Crown chakra into the 13th dimension and it will be done. Imagine your Pineal Gland moving up as far as it can stretch. Don't be concerned about not knowing where the 13th dimension is – just imagine your Pineal Gland moving as far up as you can imagine and Spirit will guide it into this dimension.

When you reach the 13th dimension, declare: "Mother/ Father God/Creator, The I AM of All That Is, I now set the intention and command that every Cell of my body, all consciousness of my Being now vibrates in the I AM of love, light, peace, harmony and awakens, knows and remembers that I AM the I AM of All That Is. Thank you. It is done! It is done! It is done!"

The reason for giving thanks that it is done is because in the higher dimensions, there is no past, present, or future, and as Masters, giving thanks brings what we would call future energy into manifestation now. When Masters pray they give thanks and bring all requests into the now.

The more you set your intention and prayer through your Pineal Gland DNA Source connection, the easier it is to download the manifestation in this dimension. Because everything is collective, when you are merging your DNA with the collective frequency of the Creator, you are aligning your I AM Source with the I AM Source of All That Is. You are actually activating the DNA memory of God/Source within yourself. With this activation, through intention you and the Source begin working together consciously for your Soul's higher purpose on the Earth. The more you do this, the easier it becomes. The universal energy is waiting to support your intentions and requests.

As you and the God/Source energy of love become one of Co-Creation, it is very important to watch your thoughts. You are vibrating in Source energy that will match the frequency of your thoughts and beliefs. Remember, the subconscious' role. If you are in the negative thought, your subconscious will look into its file and download more stories of like energy. If you think negative thoughts, your collective DNA system will match the frequencies bringing more of this negative program into your physical life, and you will merge into the morphogenetic field of the negative thoughts. Of course the same is true of Co-Creating loving magical intentions and thoughts that will shift your belief systems and perceptions. Your subconscious will work as your ally and download like memories for you to match and merge with. The match will move you into the morphogenetic field of your higher knowing and create more light, magic, and possibilities in your life.

I suggest you create a mantra to block your negative thought patterns. Years ago, I created the mantra "Beautiful," and every time a negative thought came into my mind, I would say "Beautiful." Soon my subconscious was working for me and every time a negative thought would start to surface, the word "Beautiful" would immediately come into my mind and delete the negative thought or programming from my inner computer system.

As conscious Co-Creators, we now have the opportunity for all compartments of our brain to support each other.

When setting intentions through your Pineal Gland DNA connection with Source, you most likely will feel the frequency of the request download into your energy body. You might feel a little tingly, hear a tone, feel very peaceful, or even feel light coming into your body. You are activating your etheric DNA systems into a higher color/sound frequency and matching it with Source.

Once again, the technique is:

Bring a bright, golden light from the center of your root, up through your second chakra, solar plexus, heart, thymus, third eye and into your Pineal Gland, activating and opening it up through your crown into the 13th dimension or as high up as you can imagine. Imagine this Gland vibrating into the heart of Mother/Father/Creator Source energy.

Set the intention to feel the connection. (Remember, Spirit is assisting you.) Then say: "Mother, Father, God, Creator, the Source of I AM of All That Is, I now set the intention and command that every Cell of my body, that all consciousness

of my Being now awakens, knows, and remembers that I am love, light, peace, harmony, and the highest consciousness of the I AM of All That Is. Thank you. It is done. It is done. It is done."

Remember, your subconscious is like Google, and your body is a live computer system. Your subconscious will go into your Soul's mind, files, and memories and Google up and open any websites (lifetimes or time frames) of similar experiences of your light and magnificence. When you are connected through your Pineal Gland connection to Source, your brain is actually in a state of Theta consciousness. (We will explain more about how to use Theta later in the book.)

If you are not comfortable with the word for the Source - Mother, Father, Creator - use whatever language or words you are comfortable using. Your mind, body, and consciousness want to feel comfortable and safe with your words and language of your expression of God/Source. As they feel safe, it is much easier for them to respond to your requests.

The Pineal Gland actually opens and connects your frequency to Source. This connection opens a direct line of communication and gives you the opportunity to ask questions.

After the connection is opened, ask Mother Sophia (the Creator's feminine heart) if She has a message. Wait for the answer or energy feeling. Then ask the Creator if He has a message. Wait for an answer or energy.

Many times you may not receive an answer through the mind, but you will experience feelings of love and safety. The more you connect with this Source energy and feel safe, the easier it will be for you to feel and experience yourself in alignment with your higher good. You and the Creator will always have a direct line of communication, and this link will give you the opportunity to start living your life from the Knowingness, from unconditional love. As you vibrate in the essence of Knowingness, you will intuitively feel and know where to go and what to do. The Pineal Gland is your phone line to Source. The Creator will so gladly and willingly assist you in whatever your intentions, desires, and needs may be.

Now that you have made your DNA connection with the Source, imagine the same Golden Cord, or band, move back down through your Pineal Gland, third eye, throat chakra, thymus (the new lifetime chakra), heart, solar plexus, second chakra, and out your root into the heart, or center, of Mother/ Father Earth. Imagine Mother/Father Earth putting hands on the bottom of your feet and pulling the Source energy through you into the center of their heart's love. This grounds your God/Source DNA connection to the DNA grid system of the Earth.

This DNA source connection will strengthen and align your core essence with the divine love essence of Creation. The strength and safety of this connection will assist you to let go and allow your Soul to guide you through the next steps of your Soul's Awakening journey through Ascension and into living from a totally awakened state of consciousness (Enlightenment).

∞

CHAPTER 6

CREATOR/EARTH GROUNDING TECHNIQUE

In The pineal Gland activation, you linked the Golden cord from Mother/Father/Creator through you into the heart of Mother Earth. In this grounding process, we are using the same Golden cord link that runs through you from Creation into the Earth.

Creator/Earth Grounding Technique

Bring your golden spiritual cord/band from the Creator DNA (Pineal Gland) down through the center of your body, through your chakras, and out your root into the center of the Earth. Then imagine yourself going into the center of your third eye and hook, or connect your third eye into the golden cord/band that runs through your body. After your third eye is connected, go into the center of your heart chakra and connect your heart into the golden cord/band running through your body. Next, go into the center of your second chakra (about two inches below the navel) and connect it into the golden cord/band. Now, continue to run the cord/band from the Creator down through your body into the Earth. Once you have made the connection, run it back up through your body, through your Pineal Gland, and into the Source making sure you have connected the second chakra, heart

chakra, and third eye into the golden cord/band. Run the golden cord/band with your three chakras hooked to it back down through your body and into the center of the Earth.

You will feel yourself very grounded with Source energy vibrating through your body and with your higher self as your guiding light.

It is important to start your day using this technique. I suggest you ground yourself with Creator/Source DNA into Mother/Father Earth's DNA system before you get out of bed in the morning. This simple technique will change your life and your world. You will no longer match your old hurtful emotions or stories. You will be aligned with the heart and mind of God, of Creator. This technique assists you to think and feel from the Source's higher consciousness. You are linking your higher spiritual Self through all levels of your body and grounding your light into the Earth.

You will be amazed at how much your perceptions of life will change. You will move out of fearful emotions and will experience life's circumstances from your heart's love and the mind of your higher God self. You will see and experience your life and others beyond the emotions of the karmic lessons that you agreed to learn from. You will no longer experience judgment toward yourself and others. You will love and admire others for their difficult lessons and will hold love, light, and appreciation for their journey. You may even experience humor as you witness your own mind's chatter.

Forgiveness will be your highest priority and love, appreciation, greater fulfillment, and compassion will be your lens of perception. Through this link, your God Self DNA will match and merge with the morphogenetic field of the Creator's love and higher consciousness and intention for the world.

As you vibrate from your higher Being self, your light will turn the light on in others. As you vibrate in the morphogenetic field of Christ/God/Source I AM energy, your presence will activate the collective DNA system of others, assisting them to match and merge with the higher love of Creation.

Experiencing the Grounding Technique

Experiment:
Without using the grounding technique: sit with another person and share with them a story of something that is going on in your life. Feel the emotions of your story. Then, have the other person share with you a story of something that is going on in their life. How do you feel sharing your story? How do you feel when they share their story with you? Can you feel any energy coming from them?

Next:
Ground yourselves with the Creator/Earth Grounding Technique. Now tell the same story and feel the difference in your energy and perception of the story. Have the other person tell their story. How do you feel about or perceive their story?

You will experience your two stories from totally different energies and lenses of perception. The first time you told the story you were communicating from your emotions or pain body. The second time you told your story, you were seeing and experiencing from your higher consciousness. When you witness your story from your higher consciousness, you have the ability to rewrite the story. You are vibrating beyond your emotions and are in the heart and mind of God. In this place of love and grace, you may receive intuitive messages allowing you the opportunity to change the outcome of whatever lessons you may be going through. From this perception, you may see the humor and even laugh at how insignificant the story seems.

This simple technique will assist you to live from your higher God self's perception of life and to vibrate in the morphogenetic field of your higher intention.

∞

"You have always matched and Co-Created your reality, and once you understand this, through intention you can choose what you want to match and merge with. Change your thoughts and beliefs, and you will change your own world and the world around you."

~ Message from the CREATOR ~

∞

CHAPTER 7

Collective DNA Matching

For those of you who are not quite sure how to match your DNA to your desires and goals, this is a quick "How To" guide.

First it is important to decide what you want to match. Think of what is most important for you in your life right now, what your future goals are, and what is needed to accomplish these goals.

Explaining the Process

I always start my day opening my Pineal Gland into the Source Love. After the connection is made, I match and merge with the Source energy of Mother/Father/God Creator. I then match and merge my collective DNA with my higher self. When I do this before I get out of bed, I am one with Source and vibrating in the higher picture, or understanding, of whatever life brings to me. My experience is from the higher lens of perception and higher purpose of all lessons. From this higher perception, I am able to hold God's love for whomever or whatever the circumstances may be. In this vibration of love, grace, and forgiveness, a healing takes place.

If you continuously start your day matching your higher self and Mother/Father/Creator's love, your unwavering presence will hold this vibration for others to match and merge with. Remember the collective DNA is always matching and merging with its environment. The Creator DNA is pure love and is so beautiful, bright, healing, and strong that it will match the higher self, or intention, of whoever you are around. This match actually turns the light on in others. If they are vibrating in old energy patterns and you are vibrating in the morphogenetic field of the higher Creator DNA, your DNA will activate the light in them. They will feel better from being around you because your Creator DNA will match and merge with their Higher Self and Creator DNA system's self. This match shifts them into the morphogenetic field of their own God/Source Self.

Once again, before you match your collective DNA to your intentions, it is important to have your Pineal Gland DNA open, connected, and solid. Through this connection, your intentions will be vibrating in the super conscious energy of Source. This energy is pure, raw love and is waiting to assist you in whatever your desires and beliefs are. If you still believe there is not enough money, prosperity, love, etc. this raw energy will assist you to match that belief, and you will bring more of lack, fear, sorrow, and desperation to you.

If you desire love, health, freedom, joy, happiness, prosperity, abundance, and your Soul's highest purpose on the Earth plane now, this raw Source Creator energy will match your thoughts and desires, and you will bring more of this back to you. As you match and bring your greater desires back to you, your beliefs and perceptions change and shift you out of duality and into your higher knowing multi-dimensionally.

You have always matched and Co-Created your reality, and once you understand this, through intention you can choose what you want to match and merge with. Change your thoughts and beliefs, and you will change your own world and the world around you.

Because everything is color and sound, you are fine-tuning your body's instrument into higher octaves of a beautiful symphony that resonates with the light and love throughout and within your Soul's journey. As you turn your frequencies up, it is much easier to match your goals. The higher frequencies are love, peace, harmony, gratitude, forgiveness, compassion and freedom. As you vibrate with the Creator in these rainbow frequencies, the door of health, love, prosperity, and abundance is wide open and waiting for you to merge into their morphogenetic fields.

I have already explained how to open your Pineal Gland DNA and how to ground yourself to Source. In the back of the book, we will take you through the whole technique: the Pineal Gland Activation, the Grounding Technique, the DNA Matching, and the **"Heart Love/Theta Healing Process."**

Matching Intentions

I suggest you make a list of what your desires and intentions are for this amazing, new lifetime that you are Co-Creating and ascending into.

Everything is intention. However, when using the Pineal

Gland DNA connection to Source, it is important in the lower dimensional realms to know what you would like to manifest, or match. When setting intentions with the Source, you are the link, the bridge that is awakening and activating the vibration of the intentions into the Cells of your bodies. Your etheric body's collective DNA will match and merge with your intentions. This match activates and shifts your physical body's DNA.

Your physical body's DNA and your etheric body's DNA both hold all the memory from the beginning of your Soul's journey. This process is re-activating them. Your DNA holds every experience, agreement, and emotion you have ever gone through. This technique will show you how to match frequencies, to activate your etheric body's DNA system to live and blend Heaven and Earth within yourself, and merge into the morphogenetic field of your intentions.

Make a list of what you want to match, or manifest, in your life. If you don't know what you want, make a list of what you don't want, and then write down the opposite. What you want is sometimes opposite of what you don't want. It is important to always set intentions to match in the positive. If you set the intention of what you don't want, you will bring more of it to you. The subconscious can't discern between don't and do. If you aren't clear, go up through your Pineal Gland, into the heart and mind of Source and ask the Creator for assistance. Ask Creator what they feel would be best for you, and you will receive an answer, sometimes through the mind, other times intuitively through feelings or Knowingness. If you are not sure if it is your mind or the Creator speaking to you, ask, and if it is the Creator, you will usually feel an energy with the answer.

The more you ask the Creator for assistance, the easier it will be for you to know the difference between your mind and the Creator's energy and answer.

Make a list of the intentions that you want to match. Below is a list of a few intentions that you can use. Match whatever you desire to have manifest in your life.

Intentions

Always start with Matching.
*Mother/Father/Creator
*Higher Self
This is your foundation.

Prosperity/Money

Think of all of the spiritual people in the world who are very prosperous and of all of the wealth in the world. Imagine that you have just won a big lottery. Feel the energy and excitement of the win and the freedom and choices that the big win gives you. As you think of this, imagine and feel the energy of the wealth frequency wrapping itself around you like a blanket.

Health/Healing

Think of and imagine all of the healthy people in the world. It may be someone that you see in the movies or on TV. Imagine yourself connected to them. Think of how conscious people have become with food, what Dr. Oz and similar television shows share about food and health. Imagine what you would feel like and what you would be able to do and achieve if your body was vibrating in total health. Imagine this pristine life force energy move into your body, into your cells and tissues. As it changes the molecules in your body, feel this vibration of health running through your whole body, and breathe into your healthy, vibrant body. Feel the love. Imagine all of this healthy, vibrant energy wrap itself around you like a safe blanket of healing love.

*Joy
Write down what joy is to you. Then imagine the joy frequency around you as it vibrates through every cell of your body.

*Happiness
If you don't have memories of happiness, copy someone else who you think is happy and feel the vibration around you. Write down what happiness would look and feel like to you. Then connect the vibration of your intention for happiness to your experience of other people's happiness. Remember, everything is collective, and you can activate and download happiness into your body and consciousness. Listen to and feel the song "Happy" by Pharrell Williams.

*Peace

Write down what peace means and looks like to you and connect it to the collective intention of peace for our world. Wrap the peace frequencies around you, and send it out to the world.

*Harmony

If you lived your life in total harmony, what would it look like and how would you feel? Write it down, and put or wrap the frequency around you.

*Great sex

A friend asked me to put this in the book. Once again write down what great sex is to you. It could be sacred tantra sex or whatever you prefer. Then imagine the energy of this powerful life force frequency move up through your root chakra into your whole body and wrap itself around you like a blanket of love.

*Inner crystal children

Inside of us we all have the magical crystal children who are being born on our planet today. Watch children and experience their magic, joy, laughter, and innocence. See and feel how conscious and aware they are. Feel their uniqueness and wrap their magical life force energy around you like a blanket. As you do this, you are activating your inner crystal children's energy.

*Magic

There is so much magic that is now awakening in the world. Nature itself is magic. Feel it – imagine yourself like a child in nature. Animals are magic! Movies are showing and opening time lines of magic. Feel the magic energy wrap itself around you

*Job

If you know the job that you desire, write down a description of it. If you are not sure of your next step or job situation, imagine the energy or frequency of a perfect job. You don't even have to know what it is; God/Source knows and many times it is even grander than what you can imagine. Go through the Pineal Gland and set the intention for your Soul's higher purpose, your perfect job, or work on the Earth now. Also, you may imagine others who are living and working from their Soul's higher purpose, and bring this energy around you.

*Car

Write down the perfect car description for you .Imagine yourself driving the car. What does it feel like and how do you feel when you drive it? Feel the energy around you. Feel how prosperous and safe you feel in your new car. Feel the joy, happiness, and freedom your new car brings to you. Remember, emotions affect and shift the DNA, both positive and negative; you want to stay positive.

*House

Write down how you feel in your new home. Feel the joy. Write down your dream house and be realistic. What does it look like, and how do you feel in it? What has it meant to you to achieve bringing this home to yourself. Feel the accomplishment. Feel and wrap the energy around you.

* New partner

Write down the qualities that you would like in your new partner. (Be specific.) Example: kind, loving, supportive, financially secure, likes to communicate, is secure in showing feelings, healthy and health conscious, loves the outdoors, loves animals, blends well with my family, and anything else that you can think of. Imagine this energy wrap or put itself around you and let go to allow the Source or Universe to bring your highest relationship to you. Put in your request. The Creator knows your highest good and will assist to Co-Create a relationship that mirrors back to you your greatest qualities.

*Healthy relationships – parents, children, spouses, friends

Write down what healthy relationships look and feel like to you. Imagine yourself vibrating and communicating in this harmonious and safe love. Feel the safety of communication as you express yourself and others acknowledge your feelings and emotions; feel this sense of validation. Imagine listening to others and really experience how they feel. As a Co-Creator, you can choose to shift old emotional energies into love, communication, and compassion. Once again feel this peaceful, safe love vibration wrap itself around you in a blanket of safety.

*Gratitude

The most important match is Gratitude. As we give thanks and are grateful for the many blessing in our life, we expand our energy to make room to bring more blessings into our life to be grateful for. I have experienced that as I start thinking about what I have to be grateful for, my subconscious opens up so many memories of gratitude, and the incidents start flooding my whole Being with love. My heart map opens to the memories, and my whole body feels the love of the blessings. Make a list of what you have to grateful for. Then wrap the vibration around you and bring the frequency into your heart. Take a few slow, deep breaths and feel the vibration of love fill your whole body with gratitude.

*and of course, love, Love, LOVE and more LOVE!

Matching love is a little different from matching other requests. When matching love, you will activate your own divine God/Source Love to match the purest love of Creation. We will show you how to do this at the end of this chapter (different process).

*Forgiveness

In the next chapter, we will also show you how to use your heart's love to heal what needs to be *forgiven*, both who you need to *forgive* and those who need to *forgive* you.

Remember, when matching your intentions, the subconscious will open its files to any other memories of like consciousness – past, present, and future.

Just as your subconscious holds every memory of your Soul's journey, your heart also has an emotional map. This map holds every feeling and emotional experience that your subconscious is opening for you. The heart and subconscious work together, and when you become specific about your desires, your subconscious and your heart will support the match. You want your heart to align with the subconscious download to the feeling and emotional memories of love. This is why it is important to be as specific as you can.

At the same time, your collective and physical DNA are responding to each other from your energy matches, your subconscious is Googling up, turning on, and activating similar memories of your desired intentions. So when your subconscious opens up a file, your heart opens up the feelings connected to the experience. Your heart's map remembers every feeling and emotion of your Soul's experiences. You may not physically feel the emotions of the experience, but your body's emotional memories are awakened and activated.

When all of these compatible websites have opened and are matching the higher vibration of your intention, your etheric DNA will merge with and vibrate in the morphogenetic field of the color and sound of the intentions. Through your awakened heart's love, you will feel a beautiful symphony of light, sound, and rainbows of color running through all of your body and systems. Your body will feel like a finely tuned, updated computer that runs very smoothly, easily and effortlessly.

Once you learn to match your desires and goals through this easy technique, your life will shift so dramatically that you will quickly wake up into your true Creator Self.

You will actually feel excited and excitement in being able to shift your consciousness and realties from limitation to abundance so quickly. Start challenging yourself.

When you set your intention consciously to match, always see God/Creator as the Source of your supply. You are Co-Creating your new story.

Remember, you must do this daily for it to work. Allow it to become a part of your daily ritual and life.

When you become conscious Co-Creators, you no longer have the excuse for your life not working.

At any moment, you can choose what environment you want to match and merge with. If you do not choose to match your highest good, your etheric DNA will match your surrounding environment, and your subconscious will assist to pull you back into old patterns and beliefs, and your heart's map will open up hurtful emotional memories connected to the experience. Energetically like attracts like, and you will draw more of this vibration back to you.

If you choose to daily match and merge with your higher Self and Creator DNA, your etheric DNA system will become so strong and balanced that no lower vibrational frequencies will be able to penetrate it or you.

When you match, allow yourself to feel the emotions of the match. Every emotion has a color and sound frequency. Your DNA responds to your voice, to feelings, color, and sound and will harmonize with like sounds and vibrations. The positive feelings and emotions will shift your physical DNA into like memories of similar vibrations and experiences. This is why music is so important in our life. Think of how you feel when you hear different music. Choose the music that touches and opens your heart's love. Music is the only activity that activates, stimulates, and uses the entire brain.

When you match your collective, etheric DNA to the frequency of your desired intention, your etheric DNA then communicates with your physical DNA tuning it into the same frequencies, or radio station. As you continue to match your DNA, you will instantly feel when you are out of alignment with your truth. When you are out of alignment, you can quickly change stations, or frequencies, by choosing to match and merge with a different, more harmonizing sound vibration or a higher intention.

You will feel such a great love from within; your inner music will flow so beautifully that your body will feel like it is making love to itself.

When you consciously match your etheric DNA through your intentions, you are Co-Creating or moving into your inner Master and Guru. From this place of more conscious Knowing, you can match and Co-Create whatever you choose for your life.

I AM honored and excited to bring this very easy process of consciously matching your etheric DNA system to merge with and vibrate in the morphogenetic field of your higher intentions.

This process is so easy. For those of you who are a little lazy and just want it now and don't want to go through the process of writing it down, just think, feel, and imagine what you want in your life, then bring the energy around you and match it. This works, but the more specific you become, the stronger your intentional match is. When you write down your desires, you are moving the energy from your mind into the Earth's atmosphere. You are the portal, or link, from Creator to the Earth. When you write down your intentions, you move the Source energy through you into your etheric DNA system. You can easily and effortlessly draw the match back to you.

There is so much talk of like attracts like: *The Secret,* Abraham Hicks.

"Everything is energy and that's all there is to it. Match the frequency of the reality you want and you cannot help but get that reality. It can be no other way. This is not philosophy. This is physics."

"As far as I can tell, it's just about letting the universe know what you want and then working toward it while letting go of how it comes to pass."

"That which I seek is seeking me." ~ Ernest Holmes

Focus on the powerful, euphoric, magical, synchronistic, beautiful parts of life, and the Universe will keep giving them to you.

It is really great stuff, but how do we do it? That is the gift the Creator gave to me so that I can pass it on to you. This process is so simple and yet the results are profound.

∞

CHAPTER 8

The Matching Process:
HOW TO MERGE WITH THE MORPHOGENETIC FIELD OF YOUR INTENTION

The Creator's technique brings your thymus and heart together to open into a portal that flows your own divine love out the back of your heart chakra. Many people refer to the merge of your heart and thymus as the high heart. The thymus is the new lifetime chakra that is now opening to assist you to Co-Create a new vision or new beginning in your life. Through intention, you are opening and merging your heart's love and thymus together to create a new conscious life's story. When you were born, you forgot that before you incarnated into this lifetime you chose the lessons that your Soul needed to learn and move beyond. Now you have the choice to once again consciously choose and rewrite your script.

Imagine, think, and feel what you desire to match. Then bring the energy of your desired intention into the energy field around your body.

Imagine yourself going through your thymus and heart chakras at the same time out the back of your heart, where these chakras merge together as one energy creating a portal of light. Move the combined light/love energy out the portal

in the back of your heart and into your etheric body's energy.

Imagine your own heart's light/love frequency continuing to flow out the portal in the back of your heart. Feel it flowing freely around your body as it matches and merges into your desired intention.

Then think, see, or feel thousands of little rainbow strands of DNA, or angel wings opening, moving, and flowing into your whole etheric energy body.

These tentacles, or wings, are your etheric body's collective DNA system opening. They are waiting to be fed and are looking for a frequency to match and merge with. Remember your etheric DNA is always matching and merging with its environment. Now that you are conscious of this, you can choose what you desire to Co-Create in your life.

Feel these wings, or DNA strands continuing to open, flow, and match your intention. Just keep matching, matching, matching. Continue to run your thymus and heart's love energy into your etheric DNA system as it matches and merges with your intention.

This process is so easy that it does not seem like it could possibly work, but it does, magically and effortlessly.

Just keep moving, flapping, and flowing the wings or tentacles of your DNA strands until they become one frequency and merge with your intention. After they merge, imagine your heart/thymus love energy continuing to flow out the back of your heart and wrap itself around your etheric body like huge wings of love.

You may feel yourself lighter, more expanded, cleaner, clearer, freer, happier, and more energetic.

Always start the **Matching DNA Process** by matching and merging with the Creator/Source energy. Then do the same thing with your higher self.

Move through your body's chakra system up through your Pineal Gland, out your crown chakra and into Source energy.

Once there ask: Mother Father/Creator, I now set the intention and command to become one with your energy of love, light, peace, harmony, joy, prosperity, health, freedom (or whatever your intention for the match is). Give thanks. It is done. It is done. It is done! Then bring the intention down in your body. You are creating a foundation with Source. After the connection is made, match and feel your etheric DNA system merge with the Source frequency.

Once you have made Source's connection, use the same technique to match and merge with your higher self. Ask your higher self to be with you, imagine it is vibrating through your whole, etheric body system. If you have not previously connected with or felt your higher self energy, its presence is waiting for you to ask for its match. Your higher self is always with you; it is you. Then, move out the portal in the back of your heart and match, match, match until

you feel yourself merge with your higher self's light. Your body will feel light and peaceful. You may even feel or see your etheric body full of beautiful, colorful, crystal lights.

Your Pineal Gland Source connection is your guiding light. Imagine a flash light shining down through you and guiding you safely through the darkness and back home into the light.

This darkness is not necessarily the Shadow; it is all of the confusing karmic patterns and systems clearing out as you merge and expand back into your light body.

When you start your day matching the Creator DNA systems and your higher self, the powerful Source energy will assist you to match your desires, goals, and intentions. It acts like a generator. Your own God/Source energy boosts your intentions and desires.

After you have connected and merged with Source, continue to match whatever your goals or desires are – Prosperity, Health, Car, Home, New Job, etc.

Once you learn this easy technique, you will be able to very quickly, easily, and effortlessly match your intentions. Because like attracts like, you will experience your life and consciousness shift into the life you have always dreamed of. As a conscious Co-Creator, you will vibrate in the morphogenetic field of your intentions. Once you are there, it just takes a few minutes a day to hold the vibration. When you start experiencing the miracles appear, you will want to stay in the joy of the miracle.

After you have opened your Pineal Gland and matched and merged with your intentions, it is important to ground yourself with the Golden Cord from Mother/Father Creator. Remember to run the cord down through all of your body's chakras into the heart of Mother/Father Earth.

Then anchor your 3rd eye, heart chakra, and 2nd chakra into the Cord. This assists you to easily ground this frequency into the Earth and always experience life from your higher lens of perception, from the I AM consciousness.

∞

"You are Love,

You were created in My love.

Love is your essence,

your divine spark of me."

~ Message from the CREATOR ~

∞

CHAPTER 9

HOW TO MATCH LOVE:
THE CREATOR TEACHING ME

Although I feel so much love in my life, when I decided to match love, I couldn't feel love's purest vibration. My etheric body felt a little foggy. I have love all around me and yet I could not feel my etheric DNA system match the higher vibration of it. I felt like something was missing.

The Creator said to me, "You are love. You were created in My love. Love is your essence, your divine spark of Me. You are Me. Go into the center of your heart chakra and activate your heart's divine essence of love."

When I went into the center of my heart chakra and asked to feel my own God/Source love, I felt as though the Creator had taken a key and literally unlocked my heart. I felt my heart open on a level that I had never experienced before. An essence of pure, crystal light, love started flowing out of the front of my heart and filling my whole etheric body with peace. I was in harmony with the Creator's love. We had become one heart of love. I was home in the heart of love and in total silence. As I lay there in peace, I could feel the love continuing to flow out of my heart like a fountain filling my whole Being with beautiful colors.

My usually busy mind was silent, and I could no longer feel my physical body. I had moved beyond the Earth's frequency of love and was vibrating in the Source of love. My whole body and consciousness was in the stillness of love.

I was then guided to open the portal in the back of my heart and thymus. My pure Source love started flowing out and activating codings in my etheric body's DNA system. I could feel myself filling with and floating in love multi-dimensionally.

The love flowing out of the front of my heart connected to the love flowing out of the back of my heart, and I energetically became the infinity symbol and wholeness of the essence of love.

Intuitively, I decided to match the love, which activated more love codings in my DNA. I felt like a switch was turned on in my physical DNA, and my etheric body became crystal spirals and matrix patterns of love. I became a prism of color, a symphony of sound so beautiful that my whole body was in harmony with all of Creation.

From that moment forward, my heart has stayed open, and all I see in others and the world is love. Another level of my own self love was switched on. I feel vulnerable and yet safe and innocent in this pure love, like experiencing life through the magic and safety of a child. I am seeing the world through the eyes, heart, and mind of the Creator. It is such a beautiful lens to experience life through.

In my day to day life, if I get too busy, feel stressed, or my mind runs a million miles a minute, I go back into my heart's divine love, and in a few minutes, I am back in peace, harmony, and my heart is at one with the Creator's heart of love. Once I opened my heart to my own God/Source divine love, it has become so easy to match and merge with the morphogenetic of love throughout all of Creation.

This may seem like a lengthy process, but once you learn the process, it is so simple and easy to do.

How to Match and Merge with Love's Divine Essence

The more you use this love technique, the easier it becomes. Once you open your heart to your own divine love essence, you will become a witness to your own thoughts and feelings and will instantly feel any energy that is not in alignment with your highest good or purpose.

When you start witnessing your life, you may feel, see, or experience yourself in your own life story or movie. You are the actor, producer, and also the director. You are in all of the starring roles and because it is your movie, you can change the roles and outcome of your story any time you desire.

You will experience how much your perceptions of life change when your lens of perception is from your heart and the higher mind and heart of God's love.

Remember to always start your day matching and merging with Mother/Father/Creator and your higher self. After the connection is made, go back up through your Pineal Gland into Source energy (which is pure love waiting to be given an intention or direction.)

Ask: Mother/Father/Creator, I now set the intention and command that every Cell of my body and all consciousness of my Being now opens and remembers that I am safe in love, that I AM love. I now command my heart to open to my divine God/Source love.

Thank you. It is done! It is done! It is done!

Take a few deep breaths. Allow the frequency of love to download into you as it activates your Cells into love. Then imagine going into the center of your heart chakra, into the center of your Soul, until you feel your heart unlock and open. It may take a few minutes, but as your stay with the process, your heart will absolutely open. You have set the intention and given it permission to open.

As your heart is opening up, feel the light flowing out the front of your heart and filling your whole energy (etheric body) with love. The light flowing out of your heart is the pure essence of your Soul's love. As the love continues to fill your body, feel how peaceful you are becoming. Your own divine love is clearing and healing your auric field of any energies that you may have absorbed or picked up from others.

The fountain of divine love flowing from your heart will slow your mind down and release stress from your systems and move you into a meditative state. You are actually healing yourself from the essence of your own heart's divine love.

When you feel your etheric body filling with love's peace and harmony, run the love out the portal in the back of your heart and continue to fill your whole body with love.

You may feel yourself become the energy of many infinity symbols and open to matrix patterns of love as you move into wholeness and oneness with the love and light of Creation.

As you continue to run love from the front and back of your heart, do the matching technique. Feel or imagine your etheric DNA system opening all of its beautiful colors as your strands of DNA are flowing like angel wings or tentacles and are matching, matching, matching and merging with the intention and energy of love. Your etheric body's DNA will merge into the morphogenetic field of love – love- love!

When you feel filled and solid in pure love, imagine love continuing to flow out the portal in the back of your heart and opening up to huge angel wings that wrap themselves around you and seal all of your bodies in the safety of love. And so it is.

Love is! Whatever the issue or question, love is always the answer!

∞

CHAPTER 10

FORGIVENESS

If your intention is to live from an awakened state of consciousness, forgiveness is one of the most important steps of your healing process.

Everything is energy, and if you are holding on to old resentments, anger, fears, and injustices, this old energy will control and limit you in all of your highest desires and intentions.

You may feel that you have nothing to forgive. In your mind, you may have forgiven but your subconscious mind and emotional body may still be holding on to the old grievances.

Because every injustice that you have ever gone through or experienced has a frame of reference in what we call past, the core energy of unforgiveness may still be vibrating in your collective DNA systems. These fear-based emotions are stored in your mental, emotional, and physical bodies. Your body may be suffering through health challenges connected to frozen emotions of fear, guilt, shame, and blame from other lifetimes or circumstances. You may have chosen this lifetime to go through the experience again and through forgiveness to move out of the victim consciousness into victory, and into freedom.

Your frozen, fear-based emotions are from unforgiven incidents or circumstances that you were involved in with others. These blocked frequencies may be from what you have done to someone else or from what someone else has done to you. Your subconscious mind does not know the difference. It just knows betrayal and until you release the energy through forgiveness, the subconscious will continue to download its file systems of betrayal and you will continue to draw the same pattern back to you.

Your hurt feelings and emotions affect your ability to think rationally or clearly. They affect your organs, tissues, cells, and close your body and heart down to what you want most – LOVE. The forgiveness process is so simple to do and yet absolutely freeing. Once again, you are using your own heart's divine love to break up and dissipate the unforgiven feelings and emotions.

Forgiveness Process

Step One
Make a list of every person or circumstance that you can think of that you need to forgive. Then make a list of everyone that needs to forgive you.

Put your own name on the top of each list. You must forgive yourself to be able to move forward. Living totally in the now, there is nothing to forgive; if you can't forgive, you cannot live totally in the now.

If you cannot forgive yourself and others, you are holding a mirror up to bring the pattern or conflict to you over and over again until you get the lesson.

Remember your Soul chose to go through these lessons, and now is the time to release the patterns and move back into love.

Once you start writing your forgiveness list, your subconscious will open its file system to many memories that have been stored away. You have given your subconscious mind a job and throughout your day, more unforgiven memories or experiences will surface for you to forgive.

Step Two
Go through your Pineal Gland into Theta. Ask: Mother/Father/Creator, I now set the intention and command that you open every cell of my body and all consciousnesses of my Being to all stored memories that need to be forgiven, healed, and released. Thank you! It is done! It is done! It is done!

Take a few deep breaths and wait for the Creator's download to open your systems to forgiveness.

Step Three
Imagine all of the energy from the list of everyone you need to forgive and from all who need to forgive you and then wrap or bring the energy around your body.

You are consciously bringing this unforgiven energy into your etheric body. Don't be concerned about bringing someone else's energy into your field. It is already in your etheric DNA system. As you match the unforgiven energy, your collective DNA system will awaken to the memories. As your collective DNA awakens and merges with the unforgiven frequency, it becomes very easy to release and reprogram your bodies with love.

Step Four

Go into the center of your heart and open your own God Source divine love. Open your heart like a fountain and flow your love into your whole, etheric body. As you continue to flow love, you may have many old memories and emotions surface. The unforgiven memories will start to melt away as your love heals, clears, and dissipates them out of form. You will experience your body becoming peaceful and light.

While your love is flowing and clearing the old emotional stories, declare:

I fully and freely forgive you. You fully and freely forgive me. Breathe slowly and allow the energy of forgiveness to release and dissipate the old, fear-based memories. Continue to repeat: I fully and freely forgive you. You fully and freely forgive me. When you feel complete, light, peaceful, and free, declare three times: I fully and freely forgive you. You fully and freely forgive me. All is forgiven and cleared up between us now and forever, past, present, and future in any way, shape, or form. Thank you! It is

done! It is done! It is done! Take a deep breath, and allow your breath to fill your whole body and systems. As you are releasing the old, you are filling yourself back up with the breath of love, of Source, of God, of Creation.

Continue to flow the love energy from the front of your heart, then open the thymus/heart portal in the back of your heart. As you flow your love energy out the front and back of your heart, you will experience the infinity energy of love, of wholeness, flow through all of your bodies and systems.

Your physical body will feel very clear, peaceful, and light. You may feel like you are floating.

To finish or complete the process, imagine huge wings of light moving out the portal in the back of your heart and wrapping themselves around you like a strong, safe blanket of love. Feel the peace and harmony.

Make sure you ground yourself by going through your Pineal Gland up into Source. Bring the golden cord or band back down through all of your chakras out through your root and into the heart and core of Mother Father Earth.

Once you are linked with the golden cord, connect or hook your third eye, heart chakra, and second chakra into the golden cord. This technique pulls all of your energy back into your body and grounds you with the Earth.

This technique is so simple and easy to do. I suggest you do it once a week or more until you can feel your body clear and clean of any old, unforgiven energies.

We have many layers of frozen, emotional energies that can easily be released through forgiveness. This process or technique will clear and clean out all underlying veils of fear and move you move back into your core of divine Source love.

As you set your intention to forgive, you are sending a higher vibration of light and forgiveness into the memory of the frozen pattern. This light frequency of love will start breaking loose the pattern, freeing your heart to start vibrating in love again; love releases fear frequencies.

Forgive. Forgive. Forgive. Free your Spirit to receive all of the gifts that are the birthright of your Soul. Come home now. Move out of all illusion and back into the magnificence of your Beingness into your own self-Love.

∞

"Your heart's mind and subconscious mind always work together documenting every experience, feeling, and emotion your Soul has ever agreed to go through."

~ Message from the CREATOR ~

∞

CHAPTER 11

HEART/SOUL :
THETA HEALING TECHNIQUE

As I mentioned, I always start my day connecting to Source through my Pineal Gland and ask to release any energies that block me from being at one with the Creator's highest intention for this book. After the release, I match and merge with the Creator's highest vibration of love.

One morning, while in the Source frequency, the Creator brought a new healing modality through me called **"Heart/ Soul -Theta Healing."**

The process is accessing the subconscious mind through theta and then healing and releasing your limiting patterns and beliefs through your own heart's divine God/Source love. And the gift is that it is so easy to do.

This technique is so simple that anyone can do the process. The technique is: go through the Pineal Gland into Creator Source (Theta) and set the intention for the pattern to be awakened in you. As the pattern is downloaded and awakened, the emotions that are stored throughout your organs and body's systems will be activated. As you open and flow your heart's divine/Source love, you will break up, dissipate, and heal old karmic fear-based emotions, programmings, patterns, experiences, and events.

In this healing process, your heart will open up like a fountain, flowing and filling your whole etheric body systems with love.

As your heart's divine love fills your bodies, the fear-based emotions will dissipate out of form, and you will feel a great peace and harmony within. Your Soul's divine God/Source love will transmute your fear into love.

As I mentioned before, just as your subconscious has filed away every memory and experience you have ever gone through, so has your heart.

Your heart has mapped out the feelings of your Soul's journey from the beginning of time.

Your heart's mind and subconscious mind always work together documenting every experience, feeling, and emotion your Soul has ever agreed to go through.

In the new **"Heart/Soul - Theta Healing"** process or technique that the Creator has brought through, you will open your subconscious mind to consciously work with your heart's mind. You will then use your own heart's divine love energy to transmute all programs and patterns back into love, into their true state of consciousness.

While in the process, I was amazed at how easily and effortlessly my old programming disappeared. I felt very light, joyful, peaceful, and incredible love vibrating through my whole body. I stayed in that place of grace throughout the whole day.

The next morning I awoke with the intention of working on the book to explain how to use the **"Heart/Soul – Theta Healing"** technique, I was surprised that I had fear coming up again.

I went up into Theta through my Pineal Gland and asked the Creator where it was coming from. I was told it was from the age of ten.

As I started looking through my ten year old self's journey, I found an incident where my father had come home after drinking heavily. Someone had called my mother to go to a bar to get my dad, and before she left she woke me up and asked me to get up to be awake in case my father came home.

He came home before my mother and when he walked through the door, he was very inebriated and did not recognize me. I waited up and when my mother got home, she told me to go to bed. My parents started arguing, which they did a lot at night, but this was more violent than usual. (The next morning my father was gone. He had moved. For me, more abandonment by the father figure.)

I lay in bed crying like I usually did at night and begged God, "Mommy, Daddy please let me come home." I always knew that God was my real parents (my Mommy and Daddy).

As a child, I felt ashamed and abandoned by God. I felt like I was being punished by God, like I had done something wrong and had to come down to the Earth for my punishment.

I remember feeling that everyone around me knew who God was and knew that as punishment he had made me leave

Heaven. For many years I had lived with a sense of guilt and shame and did not want anyone to see me.

As a child and young adult, my shame and feelings of abandonment had affected my self-worth.

I was very shy and overly sensitive. In school I was terrified that I would be called on to read out loud or to answer a question. I actually stuttered until my early 20's.

I also knew that I had lived before. At the age of three, I remember looking up at the stars and wanting to go home. I knew that I was not from here and that people would not understand if I tried to explain to them that I was in the wrong place.

Over my many years of working on and healing myself, I thought and felt that I had released these old, fear-based childhood beliefs, patterns, and programs. All I can feel for my parents and my childhood is love and gratitude – gratitude, because when I am working with others, I know how they feel. I have lived their story and through my own healing, I know how to assist them into self love and freedom. I also have great compassion and love for others.

So I was amazed when I went into Theta that the Creator gave me the age of ten to look at and release. I was also surprised that I had so much fear coming up connected to the experience. I was shaking, which is old fear breaking loose from the frozen emotions as they release from the body.

After I set the intention (through Theta) to release the fear, I opened my heart and sent my divine God Source love into the fear, which very easily, effortlessly, and peacefully melted and transmuted the frozen fear frequency into love.

I realized I had gone into the core of the emotional programs and patterns. I had already moved through many emotional veils of fear connected to my childhood experiences, but this was actually the core.

Because I was in the core pattern, I was experiencing the old, emotional, fear-based feelings of not being good enough, of shame, abandonment, and guilt – what do I have to offer?– as if they were my beliefs and experiences now. These are also some of the same feelings I was going through when I started writing this book.

As I was guided into the core patterns, my heart's divine God Source love was healing, releasing, and dissipating the old, karmic programs and agreements. I had come full circle back home into the love that I was created in, the love that is my true essence, birthright, and foundation. I had come full circle out of karmic agreements of fear, shame, guilt, etc. and into the center of my Soul's divine love and into the heart and Soul of Mother/Father Creator's love.

Once again through my own healing experiences, the Creator was showing me how profound and easy the **"Heart/ Soul – Theta Healing"** technique is.

It's a technique that anyone can use. By opening your heart to your own Soul's divine Source love, you can easily release, heal, and transmute old emotional, fear-based patterns and programs. As your heart opens, your divine love will flow out like a fountain and transmute fear into love.

Step One:

Let's say whatever happened at the age of ten left you in a place of not feeling trust or safe to open your heart to love. Your release statement would go something like this:

Mother/Father/God-Creator, The I AM of All That Is, I now set the intention and command that I release all fears, insecurities, patterns, programs, and beliefs that hold me back from opening my heart to the safety of love. I release this energy in my emotional, physical, and cellular body's past, present, and future. Thank you. It is done. It is done. It is done!

The reason we say past, present, and future is because the subconscious holds every memory of fear of love from the beginning of your Soul's journey. As I mentioned, some of the memories may be from another lifetime or time frame.

Take time to allow yourself to feel the energy of the release. Breathe into the release. Breathe slowly until your body feels calm.

The more you use this easy process, the healthier, stronger, safer, freer, more content, and self assured your body will feel.

You are commanding your divine God essence to become one with the essence of Creation (that is you). Your God/Creator self is connecting and commanding to become one with the Creator Source. Masters don't pray and beg for the connection. They know that they are a divine aspect of God/

Creator, that they are Co-Creators. They are not commanding anything outside of themselves. They know they Co-Create through their intentions and are the commanders of their Soul's experience. This is the purpose of the word "command."

The purpose of giving "thanks" that it is done is that as a Master Co-Creator you know that you can command whatever your intention is and bring it into the now. Because there is no past, present, or future, as you give thanks that it is done, you are bringing the energy of your intentions through all dimensions into the manifestation of now.

Step Two: Heart/Soul Healing Process

Go into the center of your own heart's divine love and set the intention to open your heart like a fountain of love. Your heart will follow your intention and command. Allow your heart to open. You heart chakra has an agreement to open to love. Imagine a lotus flower opening and in the center pure love energy begins flowing out. Stay with it, and you will feel your love open up like a dance of light flowing in grace, into its purpose. Once you feel your heart flowing, send the love energy into every memory that surfaced from your ten-year-old self. Keep sending love, and you will feel the painful memories dissolve into love. Continue to send love's energy from your heart into your whole body and your etheric body's DNA system. Keep running the love from your heart fountain and you will feel your bodies filling up with light as they become clear of the old programs.

As the love continues to flow, you may feel yourself disappear or have a feeling of going to sleep. As you release the old energies from your body, you may feel your mind leave with the release.

When you move back into consciousness, continue to send your heart's divine love into your bodies. Stay with it until you move into the silence of love and your body feels peaceful, clear, and free. Then open your heart/thymus portal in the back of your heart and continue to run your heart's divine love into your etheric body's DNA system as the front of your heart and the back of your heart's love merge together. As your collective DNA merges with your own divine love, match – match – match until your energy body feels strong and light. All levels of your bodies will vibrate together in the infinity energy through all time lines. Then imagine beautiful angel wings move through the portal in the back of your heart and wrap themselves around you and seal you in love as you merge into the morphogenetic field of love, safety, and grace.

<u>Step Three: Next is reframing the intention.</u>

Go through your Pineal Gland into Theta: Mother/Father/ God-Creator-The I AM of All That Is, I now set the intention and command that every cell of my body, all consciousness of my Being now awakens, knows, and remembers that I AM the divine love essence of Creation and that I am safe

in love. I now open my heart to love, to the safety of love. I am love. I AM - I AM - I AM. I AM past, present, future. Thank you. It is done. It is done. It is done!

To reinforce the healing, match and merge with the reframing intention. It just takes a few seconds and is very powerful.

When I started teaching people to use Source healing in my workshops, I realized how easy and powerful the process is. When you ask to feel the Mother energy and then the Father's, you are able to feel a great difference between the feminine heart of God (Sophia) and the Creator's strong energy.

To Experience Mother Sophia:

Go up into Theta to connect with Mother Sophia (through Pineal Gland), and ask Mother/Father God/Creator: I now set the intention and command to feel the divine essence of Sophia, my Soul's Mother. Thank you. It is done. It is done. It is done!

Once you feel Her presence, **ask Her if She has a message for you**. You may receive a message through a spoken word or just feel Her presence of love. If you aren't comfortable with the name Sophia as the feminine Source, call on whatever name you are familiar and safe with. The names all lead to the same Source energy of the heart of the feminine. Many feel safe with Mother Mary or Magdalene.

In one of my workshops, a woman made a great, safe connection to Sophia, the feminine, and the connection activated a coding of the feminine inside of her. When I saw her later, I hardly recognized her; she was so beautiful and glowing in her feminine.

Many times we don't know what the real feminine love feels like. After you have made the connection to your real Mother's love, the heart of the Creator, your DNA is activated to the memory and safety of feminine love. From this, you start feeling safe to let down your guard and open up to receive love. I have witnessed this many times, and every time I am still in awe of love's gift of freedom. I feel so much love and gratitude to witness people change so quickly before my eyes. I have experienced relationships between couples shift very quickly out of fear (Ego) and into love and acceptance of one another. When we awaken into the memories and safety of love from the Mother of Creation, we are then safe to open our hearts to let love in.

The Father, Creator:

After you have made the connection with Mother Sophia, go through the same process through your Pineal Gland into Source (Theta) and ask for the Creator (your Soul's real Father) to download His presence into you.

After you have made His connection and can feel His energy, **ask Him if He has a message for you.** Again you may receive an answer through your mind or just feel His energy. You will be surprised at how different His energy feels from Sophia's.

After the initial opening connection and communication with Mother Sophia and the Creator, through Theta you can communicate or talk with them whenever you choose to. Sometimes you may choose to talk to the Mother; other times the Father, or sometimes both. As you open yourself to vibrate in Mother, Father, Creator energy, you will feel and experience a great shift and balance of your own inner male and female.

The more you make the connection, the more your life will be grounded with Spirit. You will no longer experience yourself down here and God/Spirit up there. You will blend together as one consciousness of love and safety multi-dimensionally.

Remember, there is more than one way to connect with the Creator of All That Is. Use the words that make you feel most comfortable. The name with which you make the command must pertain to your belief system, not to another person's perceptions of what God is or is not.

We are assisting you to use the Source (Theta) frequency along with your heart's love to heal and release what no longer serves you.

Once again, to reach Theta, move up through the center of your root, up through all of your chakras, into the center of your crown, through your Pineal Gland and into Mother/Father/Creator energy.

Once you have made the connection and have gone through your healing, make sure to bring the Source energy back down through your Pineal Gland, through all of your chakras, and into the center of the Earth. It is important to link your DNA's higher vibration through you and ground your light into the heart of Mother/Father Earth.

Use the grounding technique. Hook your 3rd eye, heart chakra, and 2nd chakra into the cord that runs through you from the Creator into the Earth.

The more you use this easy process, the healthier, stronger, freer, more content, and self assured your body will feel. Your body has its own mind and will feel that love is its safety and truth.

As you clear your subconsciousness of old programmings, your old habits, fears, and anxieties break loose and dissipate. You then have room within to Co-Create an incredible, joyous, healthy, conscious, and free, new lifetime or story for yourself.

As I explained earlier, while writing the book, the Creator has gifted me with the release of many of my old core emotional programs and patterns; patterns that I thought I had already cleared. Collaborating on this book with the Creator has been a very emotional gift. I am so grateful to be able to release my karmic core patterns and agreements. It feels like the roots of the patterns have been pulled out of my body and systems.

I now understand that the Creator's intention for me to write this book was to bring me home, full circle into my Soul's divine essence. Through my healing experience, I was given the tools and techniques to give to you. to assist you back home into your heart of love, of your Soul's divine essence.

Writing this book has taken me through a profound healing and brought me home into the Source of love within myself. **I am setting the intention that this book will act as a healing manuscript to give you the tools to release your core patterns, to easily and effortlessly shift all fear-based emotions into love, freedom, and gratitude.**

Thank you! It is done! It is done! It is done!

∞

"Theta opens your subconscious mind where there is no past, present, or future. In Theta, you have access to every memory your Soul has ever gone through or experienced."

~ Message from the CREATOR ~

∞

CHAPTER 12

THETA STATE

When you move through your Pineal Gland into the Creator's Source energy, your brain waves are in a Theta state.

Theta opens your subconscious mind where there is no past, present, or future. In Theta, you have access to every memory your Soul has ever gone through or experienced.

The Theta state is where hypnosis takes you. When you meditate into a peaceful dreamlike energy, you have moved into Theta, or when you wake up in the morning feeling very peaceful and dreamy, you have just moved out of Theta.

There is no time line in (Theta) Source energy. When I use Theta, I can be in Spirit for hours. Theta state brain waves unlock your subconsciousness mind, which allows you to access and experience feelings and emotional memories connected to your belief systems and patterns. You can also become very aware of your behavior connected to the patterns and beliefs.

Many of these patterns were handed down to you ancestrally and were your agreed upon beginning beliefs, patterns, and perceptions.

Theta healing starts lifting the veils of your patterns so that you can act and react from a higher spiritual understanding. Theta opens you to experience life from the larger picture of the mind, heart, and consciousness of the Creator, I AM, Source energy.

Patterns are predictable, and they know you so well. They know your weaknesses and strengths. Patterns become their own person or entity. The way to break a pattern is to confuse it by doing something different. When you set the intention to release the pattern, the pure Source energy of love will move down through your crown, into your bodies, and start to break up and dissipate the energy of the patterns.

When you communicate with the Creator in Theta, your whole body will feel a peace and acceptance of what is. Through intention with the Creator, you will have the opportunity to Co-Create a more conscious, aware life for yourself and those around you.

Through Theta healing, you can energetically break loose from old patterns that hold your love, light, health, joy, freedom, and prosperity, etc., in conflict and fear.

When I started using Source healing, I could acutely feel threads of energy unraveling from my etheric body's DNA system.

Because like attracts like, as you expand your consciousness from fear to love, your body's color/sound frequencies also shift into a more harmonious Christ, Creator, I AM energy. This shift opens and awakens you into your Inner Master and Co-Creator. Your divine light is turned on, and you and Creator vibrate together **as one.** You move out of the I ME and into the I AM within.

Your collective DNA system will match and merge into the morphogenetic field of your new awakened color/sound frequencies and you will draw more of the same back to you.

In Theta state, with the Creator, you have the ability to release and reprogram your subconscious mind. You are unlocking and opening your subconscious to release blockages that hold you back in life. After a release, it is important to reprogram with a positive intention.

Because your subconscious and heart are aligned and work together, as you release old programmings your heart also opens up to release the fear or emotion connected to the experience. The more you release the fear in your heart, the more room you have to fill your heart back up with love.

If you don't know what you want to release, ask the Creator: Show me where or what is holding me back from opening my heart to love.

You will receive an answer to what is holding you back.

An example: If the Creator answers with, "Look at your ten-year-old self," because you are in a Theta state, your subconscious will open up to all incidents in your life when you were around ten.

The emotions connected to the incident will also surface so you can release them. Many times past life memories will surface.

The **Heart/Soul – Theta Healing** will assist you to use your own divine Source love, to break loose, dissipate, and heal the old, karmic emotions and stories.

∞

CHAPTER 13

THE CREATOR'S MESSAGE:
THE LIGHT AT THE END OF THE TUNNEL

Depending on which strands of the collective DNA you are living from is the lens of perception from which you experience the Earth's evolution, or Ascension.

You are actually vibrating in the Ascension DNA of the Planet. You are the Souls of Mother Earth. Many of you have had many lifetimes on the Earth, and continue to cycle back to assist the Earth and its inhabitants (you, the Cells) into a higher consciousness.

Every time you reincarnate to the Earth and complete your assignment in the light, when you move back home into Spirit, you move into a higher vibration of yourself, which activates your DNA into a higher collective consciousness.

When you recycle back again, you will have a different, more conscious role in the magnificent play on Earth. You will vibrate in a higher collective DNA system. You will eventually move beyond all stories, and regardless of what side of the play that others are playing out, your lens of perception will be from My heart and My love.

As you continue to grow consciously and heal in your own life, through forgiveness and gratitude you will break old karmic DNA patterns and a great healing shift will take place within you. As you clear out these old patterns, your whole family unit starts healing and shifting with you. You collectively start matching and merging your DNA into the morphogenetic field and vibration of higher knowing. This has been your journey throughout your Soul's history, and your Earthly consciousness is now awakening and remembering. From this remembering, you are understanding that you are not a victim; you actually volunteered to go through the feelings and emotions of your agreed upon assignment to understand, heal, and free yourself from the experience.

When you walk in another's shoes or experience, you understand their emotional mind frame and have the opportunity to move beyond judgment and have compassion for their journey.

As I mentioned before, many Souls of people in what you call third world countries are vibrating collectively, or matching the DNA of the war against the feminine. It is actually the war against their own heart against their own feelings of love. Remember, you – We - are each other. The feminine activates feelings that the male ego does not want to experience, so in response they try to control it, violate it, etc. They are actually warring against themselves.

All Souls that incarnated into that theme, or story, have agreed to do so, including the women, or feminine. It is in their collective DNA patterns to live through the imbalance using the imbalance as stimulus to bring the feminine back into balance. The beautiful feminine Souls agreed to come to the Earth and play the role of the victim. Perhaps last lifetime, or in another lifetime, they were persecuting against the feminine, and they are now choosing to understand how the victim felt when they were the persecutor. In this lifetime they may agree to open the door to freedom through an Earthly physical death. (There is really no death – a Soul never dies; it moves out of the Earthly agreement or assignment and back home into Spirit. They change addresses and move out of karma and into freedom.)

When a Soul feels compassion for another person's journey, a great healing starts taking place within them; their lens of perception shifts into a higher understanding.

As this happens, they move into a higher collective DNA pattern. Everything, every experience, karmic contract, story, etc. in this lifetime is collective.

The Ascension has moved everyone into the Oneness. This Oneness has many collective DNA systems that all mingle and vibrate together. When you have an understanding of this, you can choose which system you desire to match and merge with. Depending on which DNA pattern you have chosen to vibrate in is the lens through which you will perceive life. As you choose to move through old karmic emotional stories, your collective DNA shifts you into higher color/sound frequencies.

When you truly know that everything, every experience, and every agreement in your life is collective, you gain a sense of great inner power because you have the opportunity to choose what level of consciousness you want your DNA to match and merge with. Remember, your DNA is always matching.

If you look at the world through the eyes, or perception, of doom or gloom, you are actually matching the collective fear DNA of doom and reinforcing it for the world. You are giving it your inner power, life force, creativity, and health. You are feeding it your light and life force energy, and then wondering why your life does not work for you. Like attracts like, and if you match and merge with conflict, fear, loss, grief, poverty, etc. you will certainly bring more of that back to you.

As you feel and feed fear and hopelessness, your subconscious will Google up any other lifetime, or experience, within you of similar feelings and emotions. These feelings and emotions have a color and sound that will activate your physical body's DNA into remembering similar experiences or agreements. Your physical DNA will then open to the dense fear patterns of your etheric DNA's match and may short circuit your body into sickness, dis-ease, and perhaps even death.

There is no past, present, or future, and the Earth and its inhabitants (you), are now playing out the end times of every possible feeling, emotion, and story ever agreed upon. The collective consciousness of the Earth's DNA system is also yours. Every story, or movie, that could be imagined has been played out and is still being played out on the Earth. You collectively are clearing out old karmic agreements and patterns and shifting into your higher selves multi-dimensionally. You are holding the love and light for the world's consciousness to shift out of duality, into a new lifetime and into a New World.

Because you are the Cells of the Planet's consciousness, your collective DNA is matching the Earth's karmic DNA and the DNA of all of its inhabitants.

This is why your emotions range from every color/sound frequency of the musical scale.

When you truly understand that you are one consciousness, you, as a Master Co-Creator can choose to match your DNA **with the light at the end of the tunnel.** You can choose to match your DNA in the rebirth of the new consciousness of the New Earth. You can choose to hold the light for others to quicken their journey into the light and into the new dawn. You can choose to be the wings for those who have forgotten who they are and have become so immersed in their story that they cannot lift the veils to remember that they are also great Master Teachers. You can choose to match and merge your DNA with your future selves that have already awakened. You can choose to match and merge your DNA with Me (Mother, Father, Creator) and I will guide you into the heart of love, of Freedom and home within yourself.

Mother Earth is also ascending, and she is shifting out of her old karmic DNA and into her higher vibrational God/Creator self. Because many of you have had many incarnations on the Earth, your collective DNA system holds memories of the Earth's karma. As you move beyond your Earthly karmic emotions and contracts and into higher vibrations of yourself, you are holding the love/light frequency for Mother Earth to awaken, heal, and ascend.

Mother Earth is a great light Master Soul that has agreed to be the stage for all karmic civilizations to collectively play out karmic contracts and emotions. She has gone through many "Dark Nights of the Soul" and emerged back into the light.

Through the many different ages of evolution with you, her stage has been cleared off many times.

Gaia is the higher self and OverSoul system of Mother Earth. Gaia, along with many other planetary systems is holding the light, love, and color/sound frequency for Mother Earth to once again move through the "Dark Night of the Soul" that she is collectively vibrating in with all of you.

Mother Earth's agreement with all of you Great Master Souls is to be the stage where you can all ascend together out of duality and back into the **one light.**

You are collectively playing out the end times of all karmic civilizations that have occupied the Earth. You have agreed with Mother Earth to ascend beyond all time lines back into **one heart, one love,** and **one consciousness.**

Mother Earth is ascending into a rebirth of a higher frequency so that she can match and merge with the collective DNA of you, the Second Coming/Christ – I AM Master/God-Creator DNA.

You and the Planet are matching and merging into the morphogenetic fields and higher DNA systems of Ascension and Enlightenment throughout all of Creation.

Moving Through the "Dark Night of the Soul"

Many great Beings of Light go through a "Dark Night of the Soul" and emerge a great beacon of light and usually lead many to Freedom – into a higher more conscious understanding of themselves.

Some of these Beings leave through a physical death in the middle of the "Dark Night" to open a great portal of light for the Darkness to dissipate through. The Being may have left in the middle of the Darkness but opened the door for many to move into freedom.

Jesus' death and ascension opened a huge portal of light for us. Over 2,000 years later, we are collectively ascending and awakening into the Second Coming of Christ within ourselves.

Martin Luther King said he had been to the mountain top. He knew he was leaving and that he would not be here to experience the freedom, but he knew we as a people, or collective, would get there.

When he came to the Earth, his agreement of this level of service was already in his DNA. His Soul already knew he would go through a collective "Dark Night of the Soul" and lead many into light.

His intention for freedom of his people was strong. His higher purpose and DNA collectively matched and merged with the DNA of others who agreed to come to the Earth and be born with black skin. As they marched for freedom, many moved beyond fear of death knowing they would not physically survive. Their collective DNA matched and merged with the same purpose and mission of freedom. Their collective intentions for freedom through peace activated their God DNA, which moved them beyond the mission of just survival. Their collective merge into the God Source DNA moved them into the higher light of God for themselves and their people, which opened the door, or frequency, beyond death.

Mandela went to prison an angry man and came out as a peace maker with the intention to reunite and bring his country into harmony through peace. Gandhi's journey was also one of turning the other cheek and leading his people into freedom through peace. Mother Teresa was a great light who provided humanitarian assistance to the destitute and poor. Her intention was for all Beings to be fed, loved, accepted, acknowledged, and valued as one consciousness.

Gandhi, Mandela, Martin Luther King, Mother Teresa, and many other great leaders had the same DNA patterns. They were vibrating in the Christ, I AM Bodhisattva DNA lineage. Their agreement was to bring the collective into freedom through peace and love and for all people to experience themselves as equal.

Their DNA had matched and merged with the Christ DNA as this was also Jesus' purpose, to lead people into freedom through love and peace. All of these great Masters were willing to go through a physical death, to open the door for the collective freedom.

Buddha – a great Master Soul born as a prince into opulence

and abundance gave it all up to find a higher meaning and purpose of life. His enlightenment shifted the vibration and consciousness of the world as it is still doing today.

Oprah – born into poverty, emerged as a great beacon of light to assist to shift the consciousness of the world. She is a powerful teacher who has been the bridge to bring all consciousness together beyond color or religion. Oprah has brought many Master Teachers together to share their piece of the puzzle or consciousness in this great, collective Souls' Awakening. As you collectively bring your pieces together, they blend and awaken into one consciousness. This is the Ascension.

And now you great Master Co-Creators are going through a collective death of karma and merging together multi-dimensionally into the second coming of Christ, I AM, Bodhisattva consciousness and into your higher Creator DNA systems. Through this emotional death, you are opening huge portals of light for the collective to glide into higher dimensions of themselves and into freedom. Through this collective death, a rebirth is awakening, a rebirth of a higher knowing and remembering: remembering that you are the love and light of the world, that you are - we are - one consciousness.

At this time in your Planet's history, many Beings are actually agreeing to leave your Planet and move all the way home into Spirit. As they leave, their collective light opens large passageways or doorways to continue to lift the consciousness into higher dimensional realms of Ascension.

The great leaders who went before you shifted the consciousness of your world. People started waking up, and their lens of perception changed. They opened the door for you to collectively come together beyond race, gender, or religion. Veils of old unconsciousness started unraveling and is still unraveling today assisting you to remember that you are one consciousness of love, of Creation.

These great Masters went before and opened portals of light for you to collectively ascend through. Now your agreement is to continue to lift the veils through all dimensions. As you continue to shift through the illusional veils, you are lifting the consciousness for all to move beyond karmic timeframes and back into **one heart** of love.

Many of you are aspects of these Master Souls and have recycled back to the Earth to continue to assist in the collective journey of bringing all home and into freedom through love, peace, harmony, forgiveness, gratitude, and grace.

Welcome home My Beloved Ones!

∞

CHAPTER 14

Review of the Five Techniques

Pineal Gland Activation Process:

Bring a bright, golden light from the center of your root, up through your second chakra, solar plexus, heart, thymus, third eye and into your Pineal Gland, activating and opening it up through your crown into the 13th dimension or as high up as you can imagine. Imagine this Gland vibrating into the heart of Mother/Father/Creator Source energy.

Set the intention to feel the connection. (Remember, Spirit is assisting you.) Then say: "Mother, Father, God, Creator, the Source of I AM of All That Is, I now set the intention and command that every Cell of my body, that all consciousness of my Being now awakens, knows, and remembers that I am love, light, peace, harmony, and the highest consciousness of the I AM of All That Is. Thank you. It is done. It is done. It is done."

After you have set your intention, make sure you bring the golden cord/band back down through all of your chakras and into the heart/core of Mother/Father Earth. Use the Creator/Earth Grounding technique to ground your light with the Earth.

Creator/Earth Grounding Technique:

Bring your golden spiritual cord/band from the Creator DNA (Pineal Gland) down through the center of your body, through your chakras, and out your root into the center of the Earth. Then imagine yourself going into the center of your third eye and hook, or connect your third eye into the golden cord/band that runs through your body. After your third eye is connected, go into the center of your heart chakra and connect your heart into the golden cord/band running through your body. Next, go into the center of your second chakra (about two inches below the navel) and connect it into the golden cord/band. Now, continue to run the cord/band from the Creator down through your body into the Earth. Once you have made the connection, run it back up through your body, through your Pineal Gland, and into the Source making sure you have connected the second chakra, heart chakra, and third eye into the golden cord/band. Run the golden cord/band with your three chakras hooked to it back down through your body and into the center of the Earth.

The Matching Process – How to Merge With the Morphogenetic Field of your Intention:

Imagine, think, and feel what you desire to match. Then bring the energy of your desired intention into the energy field around your body.

Imagine yourself going through your thymus and heart chakras at the same time out the back of your heart, where these chakras merge together as one energy creating a portal of light. Move the combined light/love energy out the portal in the back of your heart and into your etheric body's energy.

Imagine your own heart's light/love frequency continuing to flow out the portal in the back of your heart. Feel it flowing freely around your body as it matches and merges into your desired intention.

Then think, see, or feel thousands of little rainbow strands of DNA, or angel wings opening, moving, and flowing into your whole etheric energy body.

These tentacles, or wings, are your etheric body's collective DNA system opening. They are waiting to be fed and are looking for a frequency to match and merge with. Remember your etheric DNA is always matching and merging with its environment. Now that you are conscious of this, you can choose what you desire to Co-Create in your life.

Feel these wings, or DNA strands continuing to open, flow, and match your intention. Just keep matching, matching, matching. Continue to run your thymus and heart's love energy into your etheric DNA system as it matches and merges with your intention.

This process is so easy that it does not seem like it could possibly work, but it does, magically and effortlessly.

Just keep moving, flapping, and flowing the wings or tentacles of your DNA strands until they become one frequency and merge with your intention. After they merge, imagine your heart/thymus love energy continuing to flow out the back of your heart and wrap itself around your etheric body like huge wings of love.

How to Match and Merge with Love's Divine Essence:

Remember to always start your day matching and merging with Mother/Father/Creator and your higher self. After the connection is made, go back up through your Pineal Gland into Source energy (which is pure love waiting to be given an intention or direction.)

Ask: Mother/Father/Creator, I now set the intention and command that every Cell of my body and all consciousness of my Being now opens and remembers that I am safe in love, that I AM love. I now command my heart to open to my divine God/Source love.

Thank you. It is done! It is done! It is done!

Take a few deep breaths. Allow the frequency of love to download into you as it activates your Cells into love. Then imagine going into the center of your heart chakra, into the center of your Soul, until you feel your heart unlock and open. It may take a few minutes, but as you stay with the process, your heart will absolutely open. You have set the intention and given it permission to open.

As your heart is opening up, feel the light flowing out the front of your heart and filling your whole energy (etheric body) with love. The light flowing out of your heart is the pure essence of your Soul's love. As the love continues to fill your body, feel how peaceful you are becoming. Your own divine love is clearing and healing your auric field of any energies that you may have absorbed or picked up from others.

The fountain of divine love flowing from your heart will slow your mind down and release stress from your systems and move you into a meditative state. You are actually healing yourself from the essence of your own heart's divine love.

When you feel your etheric body filling with love's peace and harmony, run the love out the portal in the back of your heart and continue to fill your whole body with love.

You may feel yourself become the energy of many infinity symbols and open to matrix patterns of love as you move into wholeness and oneness with the love and light of Creation.

As you continue to run love from the front and back of your heart, do the matching technique. Feel or imagine your etheric DNA system opening all of its beautiful colors as your strands of DNA are flowing like angel wings or tentacles and are matching, matching, matching and merging with the intention and energy of love. Your etheric body's DNA will merge into the morphogenetic field of love – love – love!

When you feel filled and solid in pure love, imagine love continuing to flow out the portal in the back of your heart and opening up to huge angel wings that wrap themselves around you and seal all of your bodies in the safety of love. And so it is.

Love is! Whatever the issue or question, love is always the answer!

Heart/Soul – Theta Healing Technique:

Step One:
Let's say whatever happened at the age of ten left you in a place of not feeling trust or safe to open your heart to love. Your release statement would go something like this:

> *Mother/Father/God-Creator, The I AM of All That Is, I now set the intention and command that I release all fears, insecurities, patterns, programs, and beliefs that hold me back from opening my heart to the safety of love. I release this energy in my emotional, physical, and cellular body's past, present, and future. Thank you. It is done. It is done. It is done!*

Take time to allow yourself to feel the energy of the release. Breathe into the release. Breathe slowly until your body feels calm.

Step Two: Heart/Soul Healing Process

> *Go into the center of your own heart's divine love and set the intention to open your heart like a fountain of love. Your heart will follow your intention and command. Allow your heart to open. You heart chakra has an agreement to open to love. Imagine a lotus flower opening and in the center pure love energy begins flowing out. Stay with it, and you will feel your love open up like a dance of light flowing in grace,*

into its purpose. Once you feel your heart flowing, send the love energy into every memory that surfaced from your ten-year-old self. Keep sending love, and you will feel the painful memories dissolve into love. Continue to send love's energy from your heart into your whole body and your etheric body's DNA system. Keep running the love from your heart fountain and you will feel your bodies filling up with light as they become clear of the old programs.

As the love continues to flow, you may feel yourself disappear or have a feeling of going to sleep. As you release the old energies from your body, you may feel your mind leave with the release.

When you move back into consciousness, continue to send your heart's divine love into your bodies. Stay with it until you move into the silence of love and your body feels peaceful, clear, and free. Then open your heart/thymus portal in the back of your heart and continue to run your heart's divine love into your etheric body's DNA system as the front of your heart and the back of your heart's love merge together. As your collective DNA merges with your own divine love, match – match – match until your energy body feels strong and light. All levels of your bodies will vibrate together in the infinity energy through all time lines. Then imagine beautiful angel wings move through the portal in the back of your heart and wrap themselves around you and seal you in love as you merge into the morphogenetic field of love, safety, and grace.

Step Three: Next is reframing the intention.

Go through your Pineal Gland into Theta: Mother/ Father/God-Creator-The I AM of All That Is, I now set the intention and command that every cell of my body, all consciousness of my Being now awakens, knows, and remembers that I AM the divine love essence of Creation and that I am safe in love. I now open my heart to love, to the safety of love. I am love. I AM - I AM - I AM. I AM past, present, future. Thank you. It is done. It is done. It is done!

To reinforce the healing, match and merge with the reframing intention. It just takes a few seconds and is very powerful.

∞

CHAPTER 15

MICHELLE'S HEALING JOURNEY THROUGH THE COLLECTIVE DNA SYSTEMS

After I started writing this book, every fear and insecurity I have ever experienced came up for me to be able to release. I am dyslexic and don't even read much.

So, my excitement soon subsided and turned to fear when I realized I was putting a book out using techniques that I absolutely know work and are life changing for many, but I did not have any of the scientific, technical terms, or language for them. I have never had to research anything; the Creator has simply given me the information.

I felt very stressed and asked a healer friend of mine to tune into my dilemma. He had a big grin on his face and replied, "I know you don't want to hear this, but you made a deal, a contract, with the Creator to do this book," and he confirmed what I knew was true, but I felt like I was being pushed beyond my capabilities and comfort zone.

I felt like I didn't have enough scientific knowledge to produce this book.

I remembered feeling the same way when I channeled my first book "The Creator Speaks." In writing this book, I was beginning to suspect that I was being taken through another profound journey of my own healing, Soul's awakening, and self-discovery.

My fear-based emotions started creating health problems, and I know and believe from my own healing experiences that all of our imbalances – sickness and dis-ease – have a frame of reference someplace else.

I lay on my bed talking to Spirit and giving myself healings, setting intentions, going into my DNA doing Pineal Gland healings, clearings, and whatever other modalities I could think of. My self healings started expanding me beyond my physical body and into other dimensions. I felt like I was dying, and the death felt very peaceful, even welcoming. I did not feel like a victim. I felt at one with God/Spirit. I was floating in Grace and knew from my near-death experience in 2004 that I was safe, and I could feel myself vibrating multi-dimensionally in higher aspects of myself through all time frames. I was in my spiritual home.

My room was full of light, and I could see and feel myself at one with my whole spiritual team.

As I looked around my room and thought about everything in my house, I realized that not one thing really meant anything to me. I could easily and effortlessly walk away from all of my so-called treasured possessions. Although I would have liked to stay in the Grace forever, I could feel myself coming back into my room and body. I also knew that I was not physically being called home into Spirit. It was not my time to go. I still had work to do and had an agreement with the Creator to put this healing manuscript out.

While going through these health challenges, I had very

little energy to function. My editor, Julie, told me about a chiropractor who assisted the body to heal by healing emotions.

This was also the second time that I had heard his name so I quickly made an appointment and drug my energyless body in to see him.

Through muscle testing, he asked me what happened when I was 12 years old. I started to go into, "Well, I was in the 7th grade," and then blurted out, "Oh my God! I was staying with my 24 year old cousin and was baby-sitting for her the night she was killed in a horrible car accident. She left behind three little children. I started sobbing and could feel the emotional energy of the death start to release from my body. I was surprised I that I was still carrying so much emotion from her death and that my collective DNA had matched and merged with her death as if it was my own death. I was experiencing myself in a death cycle and knew that somewhere within myself I was stuck emotionally. Had I not been guided to go through this emotional healing, I very easily could have gone through a physical death. I had worked on healing the painful emotions of my cousin Mary's death for many years and was shocked that I was still carrying the energy.

In 2004 while traveling in India, I went through a near-death experience. I knew before I left for India that I had a tumor on my left side but decided not to have surgery. I was tired of health problems and felt I am a healer, so either I heal myself or God can receive me home on the other side. After two weeks in India, I felt severe, sharp pain and knew my tumor had burst.

My system instantly started filling with poisons, and I knew I was dying, going home into Spirit, but at the time I did not know I was coming back.

I moved through many dimensions, portals, and variations of light, color, and music. I met many of my loved ones from the other side and received great love, encouragement, and validation from them. They honored me for my Soul's agreement and journey on the Earth.

I was taken into the center of a field filled with golden flowers. As I moved into the center of this golden field of light, my cousin Mary was sitting there with a big smile on her face, and the energy of love emanated from and through her whole Being and into me. We became one heart of love. It was such a healing for me to be able to see and talk to her. I felt her at peace. She then asked me to contact her daughter, which I did when I returned to the states. Unbeknownst to me until now, when I was in my near death experience in India and vibrating with her in other dimensions, my etheric DNA system had matched and merged with her death, and the peacefulness of what we call death in the higher dimensions.

When I was lying on my bed experiencing the light, freedom, and peacefulness of death, I was in the collective DNA system of my prior experiences with her on the other side. My subconscious mind had opened up to the light of her death story and my body was experiencing it in the now. I have found that our collective, or etheric, DNA system, our subconscious mind, and our heart's emotional map are linked and work very much together. They open and move us into the morphogenetic field of whatever experience we are moving through. My experience was the light of death.

All of the pain, physical stress, and emotions that I had been carrying in my physical body released almost immediately. I no longer felt sick and was actually excited to be able to bring this book to you. I was also grateful to peel off another layer of what is not really important in my life.

After the emotional release of my cousin Mary's death, the doctor then asked me why I was afraid to write this book, and I explained the DNA healing experiences that the Creator had taken me through. I also explained that the Creator wanted me to write this book to share these simple techniques with the world.

He said, "You are talking about epigenetics," and that he always believed we had more than 24 strands of DNA. As soon as he said the word epigenetics, my left brain opened and lit up like a slot machine! I felt my brain light up and waves of light, color, and sound move through my whole body. That was it; I knew it was what the Creator had shown me, and I started laughing. I also knew that I had been guided to this doctor not only to release my old, emotional story but to be given the scientific language of what the Creator had shown me.

I knew that the Creator had guided me to this doctor to release the multi-dimensional death frequency that had continued to create health imbalances in my body and systems. I also released the karmic contract and the emotional core of the death memory that my subconscious had been living out in me for many years. I felt very free, light, and joyful and once again motivated to finish the book. I also felt very grateful to move into health and freedom.

I felt a very emotional high and excited to once again experience and understand how our collective DNA systems match and merge with the morphogenetic field of our life cycles and experiences. I also felt honored that the Creator would choose me to bring these very simple, profound healing techniques to you.

Later that evening as I looked around my room, I still felt unattached to anything. The only thing important in my life was and is God/Spirit, Love, Family, Peace on Earth, Joy, and Freedom. I believe that is our Souls' purpose.

This book will certainly assist you to move through your Soul's awakening journey into the heart of your own self love.

∞

About the Author

Michelle Phillips is an internationally renowned intuitive, healer, speaker, teacher, author, and workshop facilitator. She has appeared on various radio and TV shows worldwide.

Michelle was born conscious of her gifts and always had a direct connection to the Source. She began her conscious spiritual work after healing her son from a severe kidney ailment. Since that Spiritual Awakening, she has dedicated her life to her spiritual purpose and mission, assisting others in their Soul's Awakening, self-love, and purpose: Co-Creating Heaven on Earth in all life forms.

She refers to Christ as "Her Main Man." He has been with her, assisting and teaching her from a young age and has taught Michelle her spiritual work through her own healing experiences.

In 2004 after a near death experience in India, the Source of Creation contacted Michelle and channeled the first book through her, "The Creator Speaks."

This Source energy continues to download information through her to assist in humanity's collective Souls' Awakening.

The Source of love energies continues to activate and shift the DNA of participants in her workshops and private sessions.

Michelle has been referred to as an Inter-Galactic Shaman because of her knowledge and ability to travel through many dimensions: Light-Dark, Shadow, Above, and Below. She is known as the Healer's Healer. Many people come to Michelle as a last resort, when everything else has failed, and from her work they experience life-changing transformations.

Her work includes:

- Workshops
- Soul Readings ~ Past Life Regression ~ Soul Retrieval ~ Higher Self-Integration
- Inner Child Therapy ~ Childhood Trauma
- Relationship Issues ~ Twin-Flame Healing of Imbalance
- Emotional Healings ~ Addiction ~ Health Issues ~ Weight Loss
- Pineal Gland Activation ~ Re-connection to Creator
- Cellular Toning ~ Sound & Color Emotional Healing
- DNA Activation ~ Shifting/Healing ~ Re-patterning
- DNA Match and Merge Technique
- Sub-Personality ~ Entity Release
- Heart/Soul ~ Theta Healing

Included in all of Michelle's private healing sessions and workshops is the re-connection to your higher self, Mother/Father/Creator, and your inner children.

Michelle is currently living in Sedona, Arizona. She is available to provide her experiential teachings, lectures, workshops, and private sessions worldwide. Michelle also offers long-distance phone sessions. Because her work transcends time and distance, a phone session has the same powerful experience and healing as if you had been with her in-person.

By participating in Michelle's workshops and private sessions, the areas of your life that hold you back, that create concern and conflict, will easily shift and change. You will experience great healing and changes in your mental, emotional, and physical bodies. You will shift unwanted aspects of your personality and release fears, phobias, low self-esteem, past difficult patterns and experiences, trauma, feelings of being unloved, loneliness, and many other imbalanced areas of your life.

For more information about Michelle, her work, or to request teachings, lectures, workshops, or phone sessions, go to:

www.SoulsAwakening.com
www.CreatorSpeaks.com

∞